Skilled Work with People

Skilled Work with People

People

Robert Adams

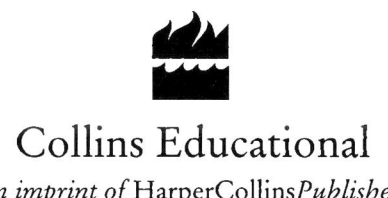

Collins Educational
An imprint of HarperCollins*Publishers*

Published by
Collins Educational Ltd
77–85 Fulham Palace Road
Hammersmith
London
W6 8JB

First published in 1994

British Library Cataloguing in Publication Data is available from the British Library.

ISBN 0–00–3223302

Typeset by Create Publishing Services Ltd
Cover design by Wheeler and Porter
Printed in Great Britain by Cambridge University Press, Cambridge

To Pat, with thanks not least for many creative debates about working with people

Currently available in the Working with People Series

Coordinating Care at Home
Tim Dant and Valerie J. Gully

Contents

Abbreviations

APEL	accreditation of prior experience and learning
APL	accreditation of prior learning
BS	British Standard
BSI	British Standards Institute
BTEC	Business Technician Education Council
CATS	Credit Accumulation and Transfer Scheme
CCETSW	Central Council for Education and Training in Social Work
CGLI	City and Guilds London Institute
CIL	Centre for Independent Living
CSC/OSC	Care Sector Consortium/Occupational Standards Council
CV	curriculum vitae
DHA	District Health Authority
ENB	English Nursing Board
GNVQ	General National Vocational Qualification
GSVQ	General Scottish Vocational Qualifications
HMSO	Her Majesty's Stationery Office
LGMB	Local Government Management Board
LMS	local management of schools
MESOL	Management Education Scheme by Open Learning
NAYPIC	National Association of Young People in Care
NSPCC	National Society for the Prevention of Cruelty to Children
NCVQ	National Council for Vocational Qualifications
NVQ	National Vocational Qualification
RHA	Regional Health Authority
RoSPA	Royal Society for the Prevention of Accidents
RSSPCC	Royal Scottish Society for the Prevention of Cruelty to Children
SCOTVEC	Scottish Vocational Educational Council
SSI	Social Services Inspectorate
SVQ	Scottish Vocational Qualification
TEC	Training and Enterprise Council
TQM	total quality management
VCC	Voice of the Child in Care

Acknowledgements

Acknowledgements are due to many people for their help in producing this book. In particular, I am grateful to Terence O'Sullivan for the idea of the continuum of empowerment, Ann Ketchell for contributing many useful ideas, Andy Stevens for perspectives on impairment and disability, Patrick McNeill for detailed comments on the text and Heather Harvey for her patient typing.

The publisher and the author would also like to thank the following.

The Controller of Her Majesty's Stationery Office for permission to reproduce extracts from: *National Occupational Standard for Working with Young Children and their Families* (Care Sector Consortium, 1992); *The Probation Service: Promoting Value for Money* (Audit Commission, 1989); *Women in Social Services: A Neglected Resource* (Social Services Inspectorate, 1991); *No Longer Afraid: The Safeguard of Older People in Domestic Settings* (D.F. Tomlinson, 1993); *Children in the Public Care: A Review of Residential Child Care* (W. Utting, 1991).

Beatrix Campbell for permission to reproduce extracts from *Wigan Pier Revisited; Poverty and Politics in the 80s*, published by Virago Press, copyright Beatrix Campbell 1984.

National Institute of Social Work for permission to reproduce an extract from *Old Age Homes* by Roger Clough, 1981.

National Council for Vocational Qualifications for permission to reproduce an extract from the *NVQ Monitor*, September 1992.

The Women's Press Ltd for permission to reproduce the extract from *Pride Against Prejudice* by Jenny Morris, first published 1991 by the Women's Press Ltd, 34 Great Sutton Street, London EC1V ODX, reprinted on page 67.

Introduction

A parent takes a young child to a playgroup for the first time. A new worker arrives to work in a day nursery. Someone goes into hospital for investigation, or for an operation. A young offender arrives in a hostel. A disabled person is being assessed for possible help with mobility. An older person is discussing with a care worker possible options for community care. A group of users and carers are meeting to discuss the community care services they need.

These are all very different situations that arise in the human services. The common thread running through them is that they involve working with people. The context, knowledge base, settings, assumptions, principles, aims and approaches to the work have much in common.

The purpose of this book is to give an overview of all work with people in the human services and to enable readers to develop as reflective, anti-oppressive workers. It provides material that will help those teaching and learning in this area, particularly at NVQ/SVQ Levels II–IV. Much of the content will also be useful at Advanced GNVQ in Health and Social Care.

Structure of this book

Chapters 1 to 3 deal with the three linked bases for work with people: principles, quality and the process of the work. Chapters 4 to 6 cover particular areas of work. Chapter 7 provides background knowledge about the context of the work and the NVQ/SVQ approach to becoming competent as a worker. Each chapter begins with a brief preview of its contents. At the end of each chapter are:

- key questions to help you review its contents
- a list of GNVQ/GSVQ and NVQ/SVQ units for which the chapter may be most relevant;
- suggestions for further reading in particular areas.

A note on terms used in this book

It is difficult to find general terms that are acceptable to all those working with people in different settings. To keep the text reasonably consistent, and where it would be tedious to list all the different agencies, I have used the term 'human services'. This refers to the entire field of education, health, housing, leisure, penal, social and youth services to which this book is relevant. I have talked about workers rather than employees, staff, officers or officials. I have used the term people or service users to refer to direct recipients – patients, clients, consumers – and indirect recipients – potential recipients of services – as well as members of the general public. References to 'the Government' are to the government in power at the time this book was written.

1
Principles of work with people

Preview

The theme running through this chapter, and the entire book, is one of change. We shall look at how the human services, and the way they are provided, need to change so that those who supply them can work on a more equal basis with those who use them. This chapter:

○ defines work with people and describes the different ways in which workers are accountable;
○ examines the values that underlie work with people and the principles that run through it;
○ considers what needs to be done to empower people and work in partnership with them;
○ looks at how workers can contribute to the support of service users, through and with their carers, relatives and friends.

What is work with people?

Work with people is a general phrase that is often applied specifically to work that involves enabling and supporting people – clients or patients, or **service users** – in the education, health, housing, leisure, penal and social services, or **human services**. The use of the term 'service user', or simply 'user', to describe people receiving health and social care services is becoming widespread. The introduction of the term was a response to the criticism that the labels 'client' or 'patient' make people feel stigmatized and put into a relatively powerless position.

Human services are those resources and facilities provided to cater for a wide range of people's needs. In this book, criminal justice services are included under this heading, although some people argue that the criminal justice system is not a human service.

Much work with people involves enabling them to manage and cope with difficulties and problems. Some of these, like most of life's problems, lack a single identifiable cause or a readily applicable solution. Some are ongoing circumstances, such as constant pain, disability or the difficulties associated with old age. Roger Clough captures the quality of work with older people well in his study of residential homes. He comments:

It is staff who are confronted by the depression or loneliness of residents. They have to live with the reality of those feelings, live with their own uncertainty about the effects of the care they provide, while at the same time they help the relatives with the guilt and uncertainty *they* feel.

(Clough 1981, pp. 155–6)

The types of occupation involved in work with people include health care assistants in nursing support roles in the health services, workers with young children and their families in playgroups, nursery nurses and child-minders, care assistants, managers of facilities in the social services, and various roles in field-work support and the criminal justice system.

Workers are accountable in many ways

Working with people involves two distinct but overlapping groups: service users and **service providers**. Service providers are agencies and groups responsible for offering and delivering resources and facilities to meet people's needs. Users and providers are bound together by their interest in high quality services. They are separated, however, by the fact that users are less likely than providers to have the necessary resources and credibility when trying to make a case for themselves, or to self-advocate, and get access to the services they want. The concept of **accountability** raises the question: 'To whom is the worker responsible for this work?' In work with people, the worker may make several responses:

- 'to the state' (through legislation, statutory instruments, Departmental Circulars);
- 'to my employing agency' (through local procedures);
- 'to my line manager';
- 'to my mentor/assessor/supervisor/work-based teacher';
- 'to my colleagues in other agencies with whom I work closely';
- 'to the service user';
- 'to the carer/parent';
- 'to myself'.

This list is not exhaustive and within some categories there may be several individuals. The length of the above list indicates the potential for different, competing or conflicting demands to be made from these different sources.

*A*ctivity

Which of these sources of accountability is most important? Consider this question by listing the above, and any additional sources you can think of, in a personal order of priority.

Putting the items into an order of priority is difficult without a specific example of practice to consider. However, the more complex practice situations produce many difficult issues, some of which cannot be resolved.

How can the fact that the worker is accountable to all these different sources – to the state, employers, colleagues, service users, carers, parents and children, and to each other – be reconciled with the goal of **empowering** people – that is, enabling them to become more powerful? There is no simple answer to this question. In some situations the worker is left to cope with conflicting demands from different people, groups and organizations. Quite simply, these may be irreconcilable. Those who work with people need to get used to the fact that they cannot remain allies with everybody. More often than not, whether they like it or not, workers will have to take sides.

Anti-oppressive reflective practice

Effective work with people must consist of anti-oppressive reflective practice. The term 'practice', which is used as shorthand for this, involves much more than just carrying out tasks. It includes active reflection on what is done.

The term **anti-oppressive practice** describes work that seeks to challenge oppression, or the unjust and harmful exercise of power over someone. This may operate at different levels and intensities in settings where work with people takes place. Anti-discriminatory work involves those aspects where discrimination against people is occurring. Anti-racist work seeks to challenge racism as a key form of oppression. Anti-oppressive practice in general, and in its specific forms, involves empowering people.

The term **reflective practice** was used by Donald Schon (1991) to mean the practice of a worker who is:

- able to use knowledge in the work;
- sensitive and self-aware in the work;
- able to evaluate and reframe work done and incorporate this in future work.

Reflective practice involves a *state of being* rather than a series of things that need to be done, or a set of acquired skills and knowledge. Let's tackle the above three components of it one by one:

Able to use knowledge in the work
This refers to the worker's ability to apply a critical understanding of the knowledge base to the task in hand in an appropriate way. In order to develop as a reflective practitioner it can be very helpful to have discussions, sometimes called supervision sessions, with an experienced worker, sometimes called a supervisor, a practice teacher, a teacher or a mentor.

Sensitive and self-aware in the work
Reflective practice involves the worker becoming sensitive to the people and issues worked with, and acknowledging and dealing with the feelings evoked in the worker, while carrying out the work. Reflective practice is more than doing things 'out there'. It is an approach that recognizes that the worker is part of the situation and interacts with people in the situation. There is no

clear separation between the personal development and the vocational or professional development of the worker. Reflective practice involves a continual process of self-monitoring, self-awareness and self-development, growing from the actual work done.

Able to evaluate and reframe the work done and incorporate this in future work

This statement refers to the need for the worker to be able to:

- stand back after a particular activity;
- assess what worked and what didn't;
- ask why this was the case;
- set about viewing the work differently.

In other words, the issue is how the work can be reframed and carried out better in future. **Reframing** is putting something in a different frame, looking at it afresh. It is a useful technique to practise by asking the question: 'In the light of experience, can I approach this task differently next time?'

The sequence of reflective work is as follows:

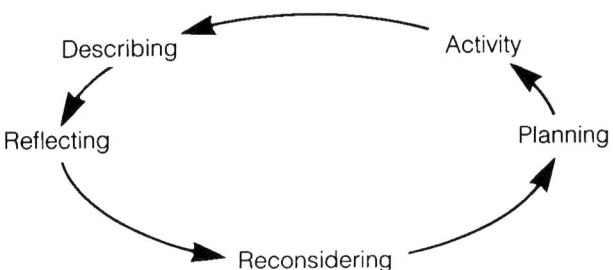

This involves:

- being specific and accurate in *describing* the work you have done;
- *reflecting* critically on this work that you have described;
- *reconsidering* your approach in the light of this reflection;
- *making fresh plans* for future work on the basis of this consideration;
- *acting* afresh.

Values and principles

A **value** is a belief about what is held in high regard. Value statements are made at different levels of abstraction. A very abstract statement is, 'All human life is sacred.' This can translate into statements made by different professionals. For example, a surgeon may say to a health care assistant, 'I try to work so as to minimize the risks of injury or death to people.' A care worker may say, 'In my work with people, I try to maximize the quality of people's lives.' Such applied values are called **principles** in this book. In other words, a principle is an application of one or more values in practice. It is difficult to list the principles that should underlie all work with people. If a dozen people from different jobs sat down to work out an agreed list, it could finish up being rather long. One of the most comprehensive attempts to devise general statements applicable to certain key fields of work, including caring, has been undertaken by the National Council for Vocational Qualifications (NCVQ). Chapter 7 of this book contains more detailed information about National Vocational Qualifications (NVQs). However, the statements of performance required differ somewhat in different work areas. For example, there are some significant differences between the National Occupational Standards for Care and the National Occupational Standards for Working with Young Children and their Families. I will now turn to these.

Different approaches to NVQ/SVQ standards

If we compare the standards for care with those for work with young children and their families, the former use the term 'value base' for care work, while the latter refer to 'principles and underlying assumptions'.

The value base for care work with adults is summarized in the O Unit of the National Occupational Standards for Care (Care Sector Consortium 1992, pp. 1–14) promoting equality for all people. The principles expressed in this are as follows:

1 challenging discrimination;
2 maintaining confidentiality;
3 promoting people's rights and choices: managing the tension between the need for privacy and confidentiality and the need to share information with people;
4 acknowledging people's beliefs and identities;
5 communication: supporting people through effective interaction, and maintaining sensitive working relationships.

On the other hand the principles and assumptions for work with young children and families are as follows:

- demonstrating a caring and considerate attitude to children and parents;
- recognizing the crucial role that parents play and working in partnership with parents whenever possible;
- meeting all aspects of children's development needs;
- treating and valuing children as individuals;
- enabling children to be directors of their own learning;
- promoting equality of opportunity;
- celebrating cultural diversity;
- using language that is accessible and appropriate;
- sharing information and liaising with parents and other professionals;
- ensuring the health and safety of children and others.

(Care Sector Consortium 1991, p. vi)

A comparison of the above two lists reveals three significant differences between them:

1 The standards for care work are based on a separate statement of core values, whereas those for work with young children and their families take the form of principles threaded through the work.
2 Some items, such as challenging discrimination and maintaining confidentiality, are missing from the list of principles for work with young children and their families.
3 Some items, such as working in partnership and celebrating cultural diversity, are missing from the list of core values for care work.

Principles for work with people

In everybody's work, whether or not they recognize or admit it, principles and values are expressed throughout all that they do. The rest of this chapter makes a statement of five principles that draw together the various NVQ/SVQ requirements and apply generally to work with people in the human services. The diagram below shows how these contribute equally and inseparably to the work:

Empowering people through anti-oppressive reflective practice

This is the primary principle, to which all the others relate. It contains two elements: anti-oppressive work and empowerment. Reflective practice has been discussed at the start of this chapter. Let's look now at anti-oppressiveness and empowerment. Official guidance from bodies such as the Central Council for Education and Training in Social Work (CCETSW) and the Local Government Management Board (LGMB) tends to use the term anti-discrimination rather than anti-oppressiveness. Why use the latter here? The Oxford English Dictionary defines discrimination as perceiving difference and making distinctions between people. In this sense, it overlaps with attempts to introduce greater fairness by means of equal opportunity policies and practices. On the other hand, the Oxford English Dictionary definition of oppression can be summarized as the unjust exercise of power to harass or crush down people viewed as inferior. Oppression is a stronger term than discrimination. Using the term oppression in this book emphasizes not only the unfairness of discrimination but also the impact on people of the unjust misuse of power by some societies, organizations, groups and individuals.

Anti-oppressive practice

There are different types, levels and intensities of oppression. Oppression experienced by a person in a sexist relationship in, say, Guildford is different from the oppression of an imprisoned and tortured victim of a totalitarian regime in, say, South America. But oppressed people have in common their experience of the harmful impact of abusive power exercised over them.

*A*ctivity

Drawing on personal experience think of examples of oppression, as defined above. Now use the following table, and the five-point scale of degrees of oppression that follows, to chart their levels, aspects and degree. Discuss your examples with colleagues.

Levels of oppression / Aspects of oppression	Individual — in the person	Group — in the organization, in the institution, in the establishment, in the family	Society — in the 'community', in the 'neighbourhood', in the 'nation'
age			
social class			
gender			
disability			
'race'			
religion			
sexual difference			
other aspects			

Degrees of oppression:

1 non-existent
2 very low
3 moderate
4 very high
5 extremely high

Some anti-oppressive work involves struggling to address and reduce one or more aspects of the oppression affecting a person. Another way of describing anti-oppressiveness is that it amounts to attempting to empower people.

Some aspects of oppression reinforce or conflict with each other. For example, when Beatrix Campbell used George Orwell's classic book *The Road to Wigan Pier* as her own point of departure in 1982 for a six-month journey through working-class Britain, she concluded:

> Being a feminist puts a woman both inside and outside the mainstream of working-class politics, which are stewed in sexual prejudice and privilege. I began as the kind of feminist who said, 'It's not men, it's the system,' but this journey convinced me that men and masculinity, in their everyday, individual manifestations, constitute a systematic bloc of resistance to the women of their own community and class. Both individual men and the political movements that men have made within the working class are culpable.

(Campbell 1984, p. 6)

What particularly attracted Campbell's attention was the way working-class men demonstrated oppressive attitudes and behaviour towards their own women relatives and friends.

A ctivity

Whether you are a man or a woman, you may find it useful to relate Beatrix Campbell's experience to your own. Discuss with colleagues and friends the extent to which Campbell's experience compares or contrasts with your own.

Anti-oppressive language
The language used to describe people can be oppressive. Let's look at some examples.

The elderly
This label can be very damaging to a person's self-esteem and self-confidence. It may reinforce a person's feeling of worthlessness. It is preferable to use terms such as: 'elderly people', 'old people', 'people who are elderly' or 'elders'. Commentators, pressure groups and people themselves raise serious objection to labels such as 'the elderly' and 'the poor'. The reason is that these terms are offensive, since they turn an adjective describing a single feature of a person into a description of the entire person.

Impairment and disability

'Impairment' is a term used to describe a medically defined condition (see Chapter 5, pp. 60–1). Some people, including many campaigners for the rights of disabled people, reject the use of the word 'handicap' as a negative label. They tend to use the word 'disability' in situations where a person's impairment becomes a negative label, through oppression in society.

There is no general agreement about the words used to describe different impairments. Some terms can be offensive and oppressive to people experiencing them. Here are some examples of descriptions of sensory impairments, with indications as to their possible acceptability to disability activists:

Term	Acceptability
handicapped	An offensive, unacceptable general term.
deaf without speech hearing impaired deaf and dumb deaf mute	These terms are offensive to many deaf people and should be avoided.
deaf and hard of hearing	This is an acceptable general description.
Deaf	The use of Deaf with a capital D is a term acceptable to many people with deafness and refers to people with profound pre-lingual deafness. Many of them have learned British Sign Language (BSL) as their first language and regard themselves as a linguistic minority group.
partially deaf	Some children educated as partially hearing may identify with Deaf people and call themselves partially deaf.
blind	This term can be offensive to a person if used without qualification, that is, further explanation (see preferred term below). Most registered blind people possess a certain amount of residual visual sight.
visually impaired	An acceptable term commonly used to describe people with a severe loss of sight or visually 'handicapped'.
blind and partially sighted	A more accurate, acceptable and comprehensive description.
visual disability	An acceptable general term.

On the whole, it is preferable to use those terms indicated above that Deaf and hard of hearing people use to refer to themselves, rather than those used by other people.

Empowering people

People's efforts to campaign on their own behalf in disability or other fields, or self-advocacy as it is often called, are often linked with anti-oppressive practice. Since the late 1980s, the term empowerment has been used increasingly to describe such work. We shall now examine the idea of empowerment. There is confusion about different possible definitions of empowerment. Does empowerment mean giving people power, sharing power with them, or working so they can take power themselves? An empowered person ideally may be one who has achieved personhood, or significance, in their own view and in the view of others. (See Chapter 5, p. 54, for a discussion of the idea of personhood.)

A continuum of empowerment

A training officer used to ask groups of junior staff and senior managers to draw diagrams illustrating where they were in relation to the hierarchy of the health service. Managerial staff tended to draw family tree-type charts of the organization. They often omitted to include service users or carers, until reminded. One care assistant drew an enormous weight and listed in a line down it all the people she had heard of – consultants, directors, nursing officers, porters and so on. When asked where she was on the diagram she said, 'Off the bottom of the page.' Where do these anecdotes leave service users and their carers? Are they, along with junior staff, 'off the page'? According to the Children Act 1989 and National Health Service (NHS) and Community Care Act 1990 they shouldn't be.

The NHS and Community Care Act 1990 sets out to give the service user a choice of quality services (see Chapter 2 for a discussion of quality). Empowering the person means nothing if it is not translated into reality. However, the achievement of significant change in the way community care services are planned, packaged and delivered will require a massive transformation. For example, community care will depend on involving carers and users *from the outset* in designing and using their own care packages. The Government's intention that it should be achieved through the development of a mixed economy of services will not ensure that this happens. Unless developed on the value base of empowering service users, there is no reason why voluntary or private welfare should be any more empowering than public welfare. After all, voluntary and private services are likely to be run by workers trained and experienced in the same disciplines as their statutory counterparts. In fact, the private sector is not well placed to develop significant initiatives in the areas of self-advocacy and self-help in the community. The private sector, by definition, is motivated primarily by the twin goals of benefiting people and profit making, and not necessarily by the motive of empowering people towards advocating for themselves. There is an unavoidable tension between purchasers and providers of services, based on finance. How can the empowerment of service users be assured in a climate where professionals and employers are under continual pressure to reduce spending and ration resources? (See Darvill and Smale 1990, pp. 4–5.)

In work with people, the National Occupational Standards for Care could be viewed as contributing in various ways to the community use of empowerment:

- to empower workers and through them the people worked with;
- to understand and empower people, by giving them access to information;
- to empower people to exercise their rights through informed choices;
- to promote services catering for acknowledged differences between people;
- to empower people by achieving effective communication and through recognizing people's different viewpoints.

The need for a range of empowering activities, all designed in various ways to shift the power away from service providers in the NHS and towards users of services, is illustrated in a publication by the King's Fund (Winn 1992). This forms the basis for the continuum of empowerment:

$$\longrightarrow$$

Giving information	Getting information	Involving users	Sharing power
Health shops Health days Health leaflets	Consumer surveys	Membership of committees	Joint user–worker groups that share power and responsibility equally and decide what services and how they should be provided

The further to the right of the continuum we move, the more there is an issue about how power should actually be handed over to service users to decide for themselves how the resources should be allocated to meet their needs.

The empowering process

There are three basic approaches to empowerment:

Traditional	Enabling	Consulting
Worker gives or shares power	Worker enables person to develop power	Worker and person are equal, autonomous

Traditional

In the traditional approach, the worker is in a superior position to the person worked with and acts as the powerful professional handing out services to the relatively less powerful person. Paradoxically, this process could put the person being empowered into a dependent, powerless position.

Enabling

The worker can move away from directing the person worked with, towards an enabling role. But the worker may still use professional superiority in power and expertise to 'nudge' or manipulate the person towards independence.

Consulting

In the consulting approach, the worker has given up a superior position and puts knowledge and skills at the disposal of the person worked with, who is independent. The worker is now in a consultative role and can reflect back to the person, as requested or directed by that person. The worker stands back while the person carries out the process of self-empowerment.

Example

Users take power

The women's aid movement includes campaigns by women's groups to establish women's aid centres and other resources for women subjected to criminal violence in the home. The history of the women's aid movement in Britain illustrates the power of people once they mobilize. Here is Beatrix Campbell describing her stay in a refuge for women:

> All the women in the refuge are poorer than men; all are allocated less money, distribution of resources, food, drink, clothing, money and time within their own families. They aren't just poor women, they are *battered*. In breaking away they aren't just leaving home, they are changing from the victims they once thought they were into survivors, transformed by their own flight into a little bit of freedom and safety among other women. Unlike the hostels for the homeless, places of last resort where inmates feel treated as if they have no rights, the refuge is a place of first resort, where women learn they have rights and how to exercise them. Feminism has generated this network of refuges. . . The refuge . . . is a new kind of politics with the power to change lives. It isn't about only opposing, it isn't about passing resolutions, formulating programmes, making demands of something or someone else, or administering consensus. It does what is necessary *for itself*.

(Campbell 1984, p. 93)

Who is being empowered?

There are five main standpoints from which to respond to this question, giving rise to the following answers:

1 the worker
2 the service user as customer
3 the service user as participant
4 the service user as citizen
5 the community

Let's examine each in turn.

The worker

In order to empower other people, workers need to be empowered themselves. An empowered worker is likely to:

- have the self-awareness to do the job;
- be sensitive to other people;
- be able to acknowledge personal feelings and weaknesses as well as strengths.

In other words, self-empowerment involves the worker being well placed in terms of external, material resources and personal resources. An empowered worker will feel confident about personal resources in the work and will not shy away from their own feelings, perhaps generated by the work.

Self-empowerment is important in work that involves enabling other people to come to terms with *their* feelings. Some people may have suppressed feelings, feelings they have stopped themselves from expressing, for many years. A colleague visited an 80-year-old man who, while describing the death of his mother sixty years ago, suddenly burst into tears and apologized, saying he had never talked about it before. Over their next few meetings the worker enabled him to express grief and mourn the loss, apparently for the first time. The man explained that in his world it was not the 'done thing' for men to cry. He had waited most of his life for permission to do so.

The service user as a customer

If service users are viewed as customers, then they can be seen to be empowered by being able to choose from any sector – public, private, voluntary or informal – the services that best meet their needs. This is sometimes called a *consumerist* approach.

The service user as a participant

If service users are viewed as participants, then to be empowered they should have a stake in – that is, real influence over – the kinds and quality of services developed to meet their needs. This may be called a *participative* approach.

*A*ctivity

Make your own lists of arguments for and against the consumerist and participative approaches.

Discuss your lists with colleagues. Try to reach a view about which approach you prefer.

Arguments for a consumerist approach

- It gives the user, as a customer, choice over which services to select.
- It treats the user as a customer with rights equivalent to those of other customers.
- It promotes the supply of services most in demand. Therefore, it is more likely than state provision alone, to meet the needs of consumers.

Arguments against a consumerist approach

- It depends on free competition between purchasers and providers and everyone having full information about every available service.
- The choice of services in reality may be limited.
- The available services may not be what the customer wants.
- New providers may not be able to get into the market to supply what the customer wants because the set-up costs are too high or existing providers have a monopoly, or because there may be no financial incentive to provide what minority groups of service users (such as Deaf people) want.
- Customers may not have the resources to buy or get access to the services they need.

Argument for a participative approach

- It strengthens the power of individual users to influence the shape of services that best meet their needs.

Arguments against a participative approach

- It is likely to lead to confusion, as the range and variety of users express their needs.
- Services developed to meet the needs of one user may be wasted subsequently, because no other user requires them.
- Resources are likely to be inadequate to meet the needs expressed by users.
- The most noisy, assertive and articulate users will have their needs met, and the quiet ones may suffer.

(Further reading on consumerist and participative approaches is contained in Beresford and Croft 1993.)

The service user as citizen

When the service user is described as a citizen, the term is being used to emphasize the place of the individual in the political process. According to this view of empowerment, citizens have a right to participate in decision making in the public domain, irrespective of whether they are users of services or carers. For the sake of clarity, we shall assume here that the citizen is a direct service user.

The following issues are raised by this approach.

- As citizens, service users must be informed and clear about their rights.
- They must be aware of the extent of rights in specific areas, such as:
  - the right to vote;
  - the right to be heard;
  - the right to redress or compensation;
  - the right to seek to improve existing rights.
- Conflicts between the exercise of rights by different individuals will need to be addressed.
- One citizen's empowerment may disempower someone else.

The community

Groups of people living in a particular area, or sharing some other feature of their lives, may form a community of common interests with shared views.

Empowering a community is likely to mean seeking new frameworks for involving it in shaping the range of services that the state authorities and other agencies, organizations and groups can provide for the community.

There are several issues raised by this view of empowerment.

- Collective views of people as communities are often reached through a democratic process. This results in majority views taking precedence over those of significant minorities.
- The community interest may conflict with, or reinforce the oppression of, the interest of the individual.
- The community interest is so diverse, has so many different ways of defining itself and is subject to such constant change that the problem of grasping it, let alone empowering a particular community of interests, may be impossible.

Maintaining confidentiality

People have a right to privacy and workers should not breach confidentiality. That is, a worker should not gossip about a person's situation with any other person, not even another worker.

Open and closed access to files

Most information on file about people has to be given to them, by law, when they request it. There are some exceptions, such as information that could harm another person. It is important to understand how files and parts of files are managed and stored in the agency and to follow procedures for maintaining closed files and parts of files, and making open files available to people.

In the mental health field, for example, confidentiality is covered by the Mental Health Act 1983, Medical Records Act 1988 and Access to Personal Files Act 1987.

Work with people in England, Wales, Scotland and Northern Ireland must comply with the Data Protection Act 1984. The principles of this Act (Part 1, Schedule 1, Data Protection Act 1984) state that personal data on people must be:

- obtained and processed fairly and lawfully;
- relevant for the purpose gathered and not used for any other purpose;
- accurate and updated regularly;
- not kept for longer than is necessary.

People will have access to personal data about themselves and will be able to have it corrected, or erased if it contravenes this Act. Under Section 29 of this

Act, specific areas of the health and social care field can be exempted from these provisions by the Secretary of State, where work otherwise would be prejudiced.

Handling confidences and confidentiality

The exchange of confidences between a worker and a service user should take place only in a situation where both are clear about how far the exchange is confidential.

*A*ctivity

Consider how you would respond to the person who says, 'If you promise never to tell anybody, I'll tell you a secret.'

It is not often that a worker can give a person an absolute, unqualified guarantee of confidentiality. Workers are accountable to their employers and not just to service users. In general, the appropriate response to the request: 'I'll tell you a secret if you'll promise not to tell anybody', is along the lines of, 'I'm prepared to listen to you. But if what you tell me involves harm to you or to another person, I may *have* to tell somebody.'

*A*ctivity

Reflect honestly on whether you would report the following incidents to a social work agency or to the police.

1 You overhear a neighbour beating a screaming child.
2 A neighbour tells you her friend hits her granny when she wets the bed.
3 A client tells you his 14-year-old son has been involved in an armed robbery.
4 Your niece tells you her school teacher has abused her.
5 A dying patient tells you she killed her violent husband in self-defence many years ago.

Write down your responses and discuss them with colleagues.

Discuss only what you need to share and know jointly

A worker should only discuss a person's situation with another worker if both of them need to know the details. A worker should not talk about a person in public. It is easy to be overheard. It is all too easy to get into the habit of sharing details about service users with other workers and later forgetting what was shared in confidence and what was not. Breaching confidentiality is a breach of trust. The relationship between the worker and the service user needs to be one of mutual trust. That trust should never be abused.

Asserting people's rights and choices

Workers should never reinforce people's oppression by controlling their lives. They should be aware of their powerful position in relation to service users. Workers need to manage any tensions that exist between what the law requires, their personal beliefs and preferences, and the policies and procedures of the employer.

Clearly, there are differences between care work and, for example, work in a bail hostel as part of the criminal justice system. But people have rights in all settings and these rights must be safeguarded. In settings where the primary purpose is to provide a service for the betterment of people, this purpose is twofold:

- to enable people to reach their potential;
- to maximize the quality of people's lives.

Statements about people's rights are sometimes linked with conditions about what their responsibilities and obligations should be. In work with people, rights are what people should expect unconditionally from others.

Many attempts have been made to make comprehensive, authoritative statements about how people should expect to be treated. Often, these statements refer to what people should expect not to happen as well as what should happen. For example, Gostin's Bill of Residents' Rights (see Douglas and Payne 1991, p. 11) mentions the rights to: dignity; privacy; confidentiality of information; free expression; possessions and money; own clothes; medical and dental treatment; exercise; educational, recreational, travel, cultural and leisure pursuits; participation; and choices. It also specifies the right not to be restrained or secluded unnecessarily, without proper recording, or given medication unnecessarily without the person's informed consent.

Different organizations – for example, the Family Rights Group, National Association of Young People in Care (NAYPIC), Justice for Children, Voice of the Child in Care (VCC), MIND and the Disability Alliance – campaign to promote the rights of people. It is easy for workers to assume that particular categories of people are not in a position to exercise their rights. Adults often assume this about children. All children should have the right to a secure (but not necessarily permanent) relationship with one or more familiar adult (but not *necessarily* more than one). However, this does not have to be in a family or a family-like atmosphere; depending on the setting, that could curb their development rather than promoting it. On 20 November 1959, the General Assembly of the United Nations adopted a ten-principle Declaration of the Rights of the Child.

1 The right to equality, regardless of race, colour, religion, sex or nationality.
2 The right to healthy mental and physical development.
3 The right to a name and a nationality.
4 The right to sufficient food, housing and medical care.
5 The right to special care if handicapped.
6 The right to love, understanding and care.
7 The right to free education, play and recreation.

8 The right to immediate aid in the event of disasters and emergencies.
9 The right to protection from cruelty, neglect and exploitation.
10 The right to protection from persecution and to an upbringing in the spirit of worldwide brotherhood and peace.

(UNICEF, undated)

This list may seem uncontroversial today, a generation after it was first published. It is easier, however, to state such general principles than it is to guarantee how they are to be implemented in particular situations. In the event, since the publication, children have continued to have their rights violated in many parts of the world.

Perhaps the choice of where and how to live could be left with the child, if they are old enough. Yet Sir William Utting's important report on residential child care links rights with empowerment:

Participation in decisions about the corporate life of a residential home may not be a right. To deny it, however, makes a powerfully negative statement about the valuation placed upon the residents by the controlling authority. Encouraging it offers them a status comparable to that of their contemporaries, and is itself positive preparation for that life after care in which these young adults make decisions for themselves.

Children in homes should share in all the decision making that goes on in families: about food, clothes, entertainment, holidays, privacy, furniture and decorations, pocket money, control and discipline.

(Utting 1991, p. 9)

Workers, of course, are affected by legal, organizational and resource factors, in their efforts to safeguard people's rights and choices. Sometimes these factors limit their ability to advocate for people. Partly in recognition of this, some campaigners for human rights argue the need for independent advocates of people's rights. For instance, two former staff members of the Children's Legal Centre have proposed that a commissioner should be appointed by the government, who could act as a focus for issues affecting children's rights (Rosenbaum and Newell 1991).

*A*ctivity

Here is a list of statements to be considered when safeguarding people's rights. Make a note of any additions, deletions or amendments you would make to the items? Discuss these notes with service users and with colleagues.

- People should participate actively in planning their services.
- Carers as well as service users have rights and their choices should be considered when decisions are made.
- People should be supported in making decisions for themselves as far as possible.
- People should be encouraged to work towards independence, while being cared for.
- People with differences such as disabilities should have the same rights as other members of society and the opportunity to live in the same way as other people.
- People should have the right to choose their services.
- Workers should make efforts to ensure that people have a real choice of services, beyond having to say 'yes' or 'no' to a single available choice.

- To help to achieve this, people should be consulted about, and involved in, planning and developing their own services.
- People should have the right to clear and accessible information about services and how they can obtain them. They should have the right to help in getting these services.
- Concern with protecting people from risks, and with their safety, should not infringe their rights.
- If decisions are made in which people's rights and choices have not been respected, they should be told why.
- People should know who their workers are, the profession/organization from which they come, and the focus and the boundaries of their work.

Legislation about people's rights is scattered through a range of law. This makes it difficult to establish exactly what those rights are. It includes the Sex Discrimination Act 1975 (updated in 1986), Race Relations Act 1976, Children Act 1989, Disabled Persons Act 1986, Fair Employment (Northern Ireland) Act 1989 and in particular areas, such as mental health, the Mental Health Act 1983, Health Authority Patients Rights Charter and NHS and Community Care Act 1990.

Being sensitive to people's identities and beliefs

Work with people should be sensitive to their differences, for instance, of culture and beliefs. Domino, a group of consultants working in the area of anti-oppressive practice, calls this 'managing diversity'. This refers in part to the need to take account of people's differences, from an equal opportunities point of view. An example of sensitivity to differences is the avoidance of asking non-Christians for their Christian names. 'What is your first name?' is a preferable question. Being sensitive to cultural differences is not the same as practising anti-racism. Anti-racist work is one aspect of anti-oppressive practice, working to challenge and address racism affecting people.

Forging positive working relationships and partnerships with users

Positive working relationships

How is a working relationship with users different from an everyday personal relationship? This question challenges the widespread assumption that, because everyone interacts with people all the time, work with people can be done by anybody. (Incidentally, this widespread misapprehension reinforces the low status of the work.)

The following differences separate work with people from simply living with them.

A consciously planned and implemented process of reflective work
Work with people is a carefully structured and decisive process of considered, purposeful, planned and systematically reviewed and evaluated actions by the worker. This does not mean that it is totally mechanical. At times, the worker will relax, laugh and joke with colleagues and people worked with. But this will be in the context of work rather than in the context of personal relationships.

An artificial relationship
We may choose our friends but we don't choose our relations. Similarly, by and large, workers and the people they work with do not choose each other. The worker is not part of the person's environment. In a residential or daycare setting, the workers and service users relate to each other across the gulf of their different situations and roles.

Empowering rather than helping
The worker's task is to enable or empower the person worked with. This facilitating role is a long way from the help given by a relative or friend, which may induce dependence and ultimately be disabling or oppressive, however well-intentioned.

Accountability
The worker is accountable to their employer, whereas the relative or neighbour may be guided by personal inclinations.

Positive involvement
The above factors contribute to workers adopting a 'detached involvement' in their work with people. This is a rather self-contradictory expression. It conveys the tension felt by workers between developing a warm and supportive rapport with a person and bearing in mind continuously that this is part of a professional rather than a personal relationship.

It could be argued that all positive working relationships contribute in some way towards the purpose of empowering people. Positive working relationships depend on knowledge of, and skills in, interacting with people, both individually and in groups. Positive work depends on two aspects of reflective practice touched on earlier in this chapter, namely sensitivity and self-awareness.

Sensitivity
Communication between people depends to some extent on the senses each person uses, and this is implied in the use of the word 'sensitivity'. Some or all of the following senses will play a part:

- facial expression;
- body language;
- speech.

Self-awareness
Self-awareness involves the worker not just in thinking honestly but also in being prepared to let feelings surface. They must then be able to discuss these feelings with colleagues and line managers, so that the personal reactions con-

tribute to, rather than obstruct, the work. In this sense, work with people is very un-British and "non-macho". It is un-British because many people have been brought up not to express their feelings. It is non-macho because many people regard admitting feelings as a non-masculine thing to do.

Activity

In a group of male and female workers, discuss differences in the way men and women work together. Form pairs, first of workers of the same sex, then of different sexes. Ask the following questions of each other in turn.

When at work, do you chat about non-work things, such as your friends, family, yourself, your activities, problems? When did you last cry at home and at work? What was it over? Do you feel that crying is OK in such a situation for a man, and for a woman?

Activity

The skills involved in working with children are illustrated in two contrasting situations, described below.

Maureen sat at the front of the room and from time to time looked up from the paperwork she was doing on her knee and made a comment to one or other of the children playing around her. She had a work-experience student sitting alongside her, to whom she made occasional comments, without looking at him.

Pia sat on a floor cushion, among a group of children. She was arranging some toys with two of them, but looked up and around frequently, smiling at other children, making eye contact with some and speaking to others. She listened for, and responded to, the numerous comments and questions from children running up to her, from time to time.

Note down the ways in which Maureen and Pia are working differently. Which approach is closest to your own? Which approach is more desirable? Discuss your notes with colleagues.

More likely than not, the worker will not always have the luxury of being able to plan a piece of work with people and then carry it out. Time and again, the worker will be pitched into the middle of an existing situation and will have to work out what to do next. The realities of work with people dictate that the worker becomes competent in making the best use of relationships developed in such 'found' situations, rather than in artificial ones. The skills the worker will need will therefore tend to be based on working in as purposeful a way as possible while making the most of an existing situation. At the same time, it may be necessary for the worker to deal with various aspects of oppression, such as racism, sexual harassment, coping with scarce resources, and dealing with changes and uncertainties in the situation.

A*ctivity*

Use your interaction with a person as the basis for considering the various issues raised here. Use these questions as the starting point.

- Are you listening to the person with whom you are working?
- Are you encouraging the person to tell you what they really feel?

Positive work with people is not simply a case of looking after them. It involves actively promoting their development. This depends on being able to draw on an understanding of their developmental needs and to use a range of skills in working with them.

Effective communication skills are part of the range of competencies needed for good working relationships with people. Many of these skills are second nature to people. They involve using the senses of taste, touch, hearing, sight and smell. As soon as babies are born they begin to interact with people, using movement and facial expression. As they grow older, they use different means of communication. They rely more on speech, for example. Not all changes in people's patterns of interaction are of their own choosing. Some people experience hearing loss as they grow older. People may be born with, or experience gradually or suddenly, the loss of their hearing or sight. The worker also will be subject to sensory differences. Such differences will affect the pattern of interaction between people and the skills on which the workers will need to draw in work with them. Sometimes signing and touching will be necessary skills for workers who have physical impairments.

Good quality interaction

Two easily recognized features of effective interaction are:

- good communication;
- indications, verbal and non-verbal, that the people involved are each getting satisfaction from the interaction.

Effective interaction is also dependent on the worker's:

- sensitivity to what the other person is saying/thinking/feeling;
- the worker's self-awareness, in terms of their reactions, thoughts and feelings.

The basic reflective skills of the worker are built on these two aspects.

Listening and self-disclosure

A worker should listen and respond sensitively and reflectively to people worked with. If the working relationship goes on for any length of time, it is more likely to involve exchanges of information and feelings. When a worker shares their own experiences with a person, this is called **self-disclosure**. Self-disclosure can be used by the worker to increase the ability of the person worked with to cope with a situation. Self-disclosure makes the worker more vulnerable. But this works both ways.

The power of the worker

When the worker shares anger as well as vulnerability with people, this is a significant demonstration of trust and respect. In work with children, for instance, it opens up the possibility of children helping adults with their feelings. When adults let children know how they feel, it is a powerful and courageous gesture, but it is also potentially oppressive. Both as worker and as adult, the professional is more powerful than the child. It is easy to abuse this power.

The worker should not spring a new situation or activity on a person. Any change in their situation, or fresh demands made upon them, must be anticipated and discussed with them. There should be time to allow the person to express any reactions, including strong but reserved emotions. In the process, the worker can assess how far the proposed change will be accepted by the person.

The worker should practise the art of speaking without confronting needlessly, laying down the law, or making authoritative announcements to which there is no answer, let alone a way of questioning or challenging them. Confrontation may tend to produce resistance and a refusal to cooperate. There should be room for the person worked with to disagree and put a different view forward without feeling awkward.

Not preferred	Preferred
'I want you to . . . '	Do you think you can . . . ' 'Can you . . . '
'Now do this . . . '	'How would you feel about . . . ' 'How would you react if I . . . '
'You must . . . '	'What would you do if I . . . '

*A*ctivity

Visiting a hospital ward, a colleague overheard a group of nurses and auxiliary staff chatting together. One asked, 'Has that lung in Room 4 gone out yet?'
  Make notes on the principal issues this remark raises for you. Then read on.

Here are some general responses. The question violates several principles of work with people. It is similar to the residential worker going off duty at night, who is overheard by residents saying to the night staff member: 'There are four bodies asleep in that room.' What conclusions will people draw about the value attached to residents or patients if they overhear such remarks? There is a need:

- to be sensitive to people;
- not to label people;
- not to talk down to people;

- not to talk about people as if they aren't there;
- not to talk for people as if they can't speak up for themselves;
- not to talk as though people are *objects*.

Working in partnerships with users

The idea of partnership is problematic, for two main reasons.

1 Partnership involves two parties working together. It is based on the notion that each is, to an extent, dependent on the other. Because of that, it starts from a more restricted situation than the person who is already empowered and independent (see Chapter 6, p. 66–7, for a discussion of this). At one extreme, there is activity involving imposing things on people. At the other extreme, there is activity by people who are already empowered and independent. In between, there may be a range of partnerships, that is, working jointly with people with them having more power, with power shared equally or with the worker having more power.

2 The NHS and Community Care Act 1990 radically changed the idea of partnership as it applies to the collaboration between organizations to deliver services. Prior to the 1990s, the emphasis was on statutory health and social services, for example, working alongside each other as managers and providers of services. From the early 1990s, health authorities and local authority social services departments were slimmed down. The remaining staff, with some exceptions such as child care and child protection work in some authorities, concentrated on becoming purchasers of services from the providers – including voluntary and independent agencies.

Some workers find it hard to shift their thinking towards working jointly with people. The following statement by the influential Utting Report, on residential child care, is about partnership: 'Children should be asked to live in residential homes on the basis that this is a positive and jointly considered choice' (Utting 1991, p. 9).

The most obvious example of partnership with service users is the delivery of community care services. Essentially, partnership involves workers doing things *with* people, rather than *to* them.

Traditional approach	Work in partnership
Assessment of people	Assessment with people
Planning care	Planning care with people
Implementing care plans	Implementing care plans with people
Evaluating care plans	Evaluating care plans with people

Most work *with* people involves both doing things *to* service users and doing things *with* them. The worker should try as far as possible to work *with* service users, that is, moving from the first items on the following list to later ones.

- Imposing: the worker does things to the service user without informed consent.
- Informing: the worker makes the decision and tells the service user.
- Consulting: the worker asks the service user for views and makes a decision.
- Partnership: the worker has more power than the service user.
- Partnership: the service user and the worker have equal power.
- Partnership: the service user has more power than the worker.
- Independent, empowered service user: there is no involvement by the worker.

Key questions

Use these questions to check back over the material covered in the chapter and assess your grasp of it, before moving on. Discuss the questions, and responses to them, with colleagues and tutors.

○ What are the main principles underlying work with people?
○ What is meant by 'anti-oppressive practice'?
○ What is meant by the term 'reflective work'?
○ What makes for an effective working relationship between the worker and the person worked with?

Relevant GNVQ/SNVQ and NVQ/SVQ Units

The material in this chapter will help with preparation for the following Health and Social Care GNVQ/SNVQ Units

Advanced Level:
   Unit 1 – Access, equal opportunity and client rights
   Unit 2 – Interpersonal interaction

and NVQ/SVQ Units from the following National Occupational Standards for Care:

Value Base Unit 0 – Promote equality for all individuals
for Working with Young Children:
   integrated into standards in general

Further reading

On anti-oppressive work
Thompson, N. (1993) *Anti-discriminatory Practice*, London: Macmillan.

On anti-oppressive work in the areas of impairment and disability
Stevens, A. (ed.) (1993) *Back From the Wellhouse: Discussion Papers on Sensory Impairment and Training in Community Care Services*, London: Central Council for Education and Training in Social Work.

On anti-racist work
Dominelli, L. (1988) *Anti-Racist Social Work*, London: Macmillan.

Gambe, D., Gomes, J., Kapur, V., Rangel, M. and Stubbs, P., *Improving Practice with Children and Families: A Training Manual*, Antiracist Social Work Education (CD) series, No. 2, London: Central Council for Education and Training in Social Work. (There are seven published and planned titles in this invaluable series.)

On aspects of oppression, particularly social class and gender
Campbell, B. (1984) *Wigan Pier Revisited: Poverty and Politics in the 80s*, London: Virago.

On empowerment
Adams, R. (1990) *Self-help, Social Work and Empowerment*, London: Macmillan.
Beresford, P. and Croft, S. (1993) *Citizen Involvement: A Practical Guide for Change*, London: Macmillan.
Clark, M. and Stewart, J. (1992) *Citizens and Local Democracy: Empowerment – A Theme for the 1990s*, London: Local Government Management Board.

On partnership
Winn, L. (ed.) (1992) *Power to the People: The Key to Responsive Services in Health and Social Care*, London: King's Fund.

The National Children's Bureau has published many pamphlets, resource packs and books on this subject. Its updated publication list will be available from the address at the end of this book.

On reflective practice
Schon, D.A. (1991) *The Reflective Practitioner: How Professionals Think in Action*, Aldershot: Avebury.

On work with users
The User-centred Services Group (1993) *Building Bridges Between People Who Use and People Who Provide Services*, London: National Institute for Social Work.

2
Quality work with people

Preview

A feature of government policy is an emphasis on the right of people to receive quality services. NVQs/SVQs may contribute to a system of quality assurance. Workers may also contribute to assuring the quality of services provided in several ways:

○ by adhering to quality standards, which should be specified in contracts and maintained through the process of the work;
○ by contributing to processes of registration and inspection of residential homes and other services, such as child-minding;
○ by taking action to deal with shortcomings in services, directly (through 'whistle-blowing') and indirectly (through ensuring that complaints are made and responded to according to procedures).

This chapter deals in turn with each of these important ingredients of quality assurance of services. Firstly it deals with the question of what quality assurance is and what it involves.

Quality assurance refers to processes that aim to ensure that quality is built into services. **Quality control** is an aspect of quality assurance. It involves systematically monitoring services. **Total quality management** (TQM) refers to an approach to quality assurance that emphasizes the creation of a culture in which everyone in the organization is concerned with quality. Some people talk of a **quality system,** which involves everyone in the organization in the process of quality control.

What does quality assurance involve?

Assuring the quality of a service involves:

• identifying the person(s) for whom the service is provided;
• specifying what the purpose of the service is and the values expressed in it;
• specifying the aim of carrying out the service;
• determining the indicators to be used in judging the level and quality of the service;

- checking with service users – and, where appropriate, carers, relatives or friends – their understanding of the responses to the above questions;
- comparing them with the service providers' views of the service delivered.

Since the late 1980s, government-led initiatives in raising awareness about delivering quality services have not been restricted to health and social care. They have extended throughout the human services.

All members of the organization should be responsible for quality assurance and not just the staff with particular responsibility for it. Quality in a particular service should be defined in the first place by service users themselves. Quality assurance should be considered at the start of any work done with people. This is because issues associated with making judgements about the quality of services – or evaluating them – are sometimes considered too late, when the work is well under way. These issues should be considered at the planning stage and throughout the process of the work (hence the placing of this chapter near the start of this book).

A **quality standard** refers to the level and quality of performance required in the delivery of a service. This is not fixed but will change as conditions alter. Quality itself is a relative term. The British Standards Institute (BSI) definition in BSI Standard 4778 (*BSI Handbook 22* 1990) indicates that judgements about quality are based not on objective fixed criteria but on service users' perceptions of how far a service meets their needs.

A very good example of a publication aimed at quality assurance by staff is the Audit Commission report on the probation service (Audit Commission 1989). It was published in 1989, in the light of the Government Green Paper, *Punishment, Custody and the Community* (Home Office 1988). The Audit Commission builds on the probation service *Statement of National Objectives and Priorities* by the Home Office and produces a very useful model for managing quality assurance (Audit Commission 1989, p. 53), which can be applied to services more generally:

1 Identify the KEY AREAS of all managers and workers in the organization
  This key area of work with people is . . .
2 Define the AIM of each key area
  The aim of this key area is . . .
3 Specify KEY TASKS for each key area
  The key tasks for this key area are . . .
  [I suggest you keep the list down to three or four at most]
4 Determine TARGETS for each key task
  The targets for this key task for the year ending 31 December 19. . . [attach target dates to each] are . . .
5 Determine ACTION PLAN for achieving each target
  The plan to enable us to achieve this target is as follows:
  [attach target dates to each item in the plan]
6 Check each stage of the action plan against performance standards
  Performance standards is a term referring to the criteria against which work may be judged.
7 Further control is achieved by regular monitoring.

Setting standards for services

Standards for services are regarded in many settings as inseparable from an overall approach to quality.

The British Standards Institution has set the UK standard for quality assurance systems, in what is called British Standard (BS) 5750. This includes a series of standards, which providers may apply for, as endorsements of their services and/or products. The standards cover all aspects of the process of provision, from determining and defining needs, through to checking with users how satisfied they are with the end-product or service. BS 5750 is being introduced in some areas: for example, the mental health services provided by Bradford Social Services Department (*Community Care Plan* January 1992, 6.26). BS 5750 requires that such services should be:

- generated through wide consultation with service providers, users, carers and practitioners;
- as readily understandable by users as by workers.

Criteria for assuring quality

Three key ways in which quality is assured are:

1 by the inclusion of criteria by which quality standards of a given service will be judged;
2 the registration and inspection of providers;
3 monitoring actions of workers and views of persons and carers.

Purchasers of services, such as the social services department, will need to check directly what workers are doing and to ask service users for their views and experiences. Nowadays dissatisfied service users are more likely than formerly to be encouraged to complain.

Registration and inspection

Inspection procedures are becoming a built-in feature of many aspects of the human services. The NHS and Community Care Act 1990 and the Children Act 1989 require that registration and inspection services of the social services department are established so as to be independent of the management and operation of the department. Since the 1980s, registration and inspection of services, such as residential homes, have become increasingly important and demanding tasks for local authorities. There are two main reasons for this:

1 Legislation, notably the Registered Homes Act 1984 and the NHS and Community Care Act 1990, has given powers to local authority inspectors based in 'arm's length' inspection units – so called because they are based outside the direct line management of the services they are likely to inspect.
2 There has been a great expansion in the numbers and types of establishments in the voluntary and private sectors of health and social care.

Registration involves listing approved facilities that meet a required standard of service provision. Registration and de-registration decisions will normally be taken by staff in the relevant statutory sector of the service. Under the NHS and Community Care Act 1990, a Resident Care Standards Advisory Committee has been set up in each locality. Membership includes people from a wide range of interests in residential care.

Inspection is a general term that describes a range of activities involved in the monitoring and evaluation of services, in order to make judgements about their quality. Inspection may be informal or formal. Informal inspection does not follow standard or recognized procedures. Formal inspection, however, should be made using specified criteria, known to users, providers and inspectors.

Inspection used to be regarded as a negative, punishing experience. Nowadays, it is moving towards being a process that can support workers and users in their efforts to improve the quality of services. This movement is helped by seeing inspection as involving two separate but related processes: monitoring and evaluation. **Monitoring** involves reviewing the work while it is going on. This is sometimes called a 'formative' judgement. **Evaluation** involves summarizing judgements at a particular time, or at the end of a period of work. It is sometimes called 'summative'.

It is important to recognize that users and carers should feed into both monitoring and evaluation. This is a central feature of proper quality assurance. At its best, inspection, whether formal or informal, should be:

- based on published standards of services;
- non-discriminatory;
- impartial;
- visible;
- consistent with users' experiences and needs.

When planning or otherwise becoming involved in a formal inspection, it may be helpful to read some of the official publications. For example, in the field of home care services, the Social Services Inspectorate (SSI) has published a number of reports of particular inspections (SSI 1987a; SSI 1988a; SSI 1989a) and a general guide to inspection (SSI 1990a).

Making complaints

Since the 1980s, there has been growing concern about the need for strengthened, and in some cases new, provision for workers and service users alike to make complaints about services. This is linked to the argument that service users and carers, in particular, should be able to get ready access to information, including leaflets detailing their rights. Guidelines issued by the Department of Health in 1993 are intended to encourage complaints by staff (often called whistle-blowing), and to provide protection from reprisals from colleagues and employers. Workers often feel that, while there is formal support, informally they are discriminated against for criticizing the work of colleagues and employers. Yet such a self-critical approach among the workforce is at the heart of the principles of reflective practice and can only help in providing a high quality service.

Even legislation may not be sufficient in encouraging complaints. In 1992 there was an important critical review of residential child care by Sir William Utting, following widespread concern about the abuse of children subjected to a much criticized system of behavioural control called 'pin-down', in some children's homes in Staffordshire. The Utting Report recognizes that the Children Act 1989 makes new and comprehensive provision for dealing with complaints. But it argues that young people 'may not be able to crystallize their feelings into an issue as clear cut as a complaint'. The Report recognizes that the new system of independent visitors (Schedule 2, Para. 17, Children Act 1989) should be extended to cover complaints. Also, local authority associations should consider offering an independent adjudication service in cases where there is a dispute between a child and the authority (Utting 1991, pp. 9–10).

Authorities increasingly tend to publish Charters of Rights of users of services. These usually specify how people can make complaints. Procedures normally involve going through a sequence of complaints, working through the hierarchy as follows:

- to the worker normally dealt with;
- to the local manager;
- to the area director;
- to the director of the service as a whole;
- to the committee or board that manages the service, perhaps through elected members of a local government or health authority committee.

Service users who are still dissatisfied have the right to complain to the local ombudsman, whose address is at the end of this book.

Key questions

Use these questions to check back over the material covered in the chapter and assess your grasp of it, before moving on. Discuss the questions, and responses to them, with colleagues and tutors.

○ How would you define quality assurance?
○ How would you distinguish monitoring and evaluation?
○ How would you advise a person to go about making a complaint about an aspect of services received?

Relevant GNVQ/SNVQ and NVQ/SVQ Units

The material in this chapter will help with preparation for the following Health and Social Care GNVQ/SNVQ Units

Advanced Level:
   Unit 7 – Care plans
   and NVQ/SVQ Units from the following National Occupational Standards
for Caring:
   Key Role V – Contribute to the planning, delivery and evaluation of services which
            provide support and care
for Working with Young Children
   applicable into standards in general

Further reading

On quality assurance
Kelly, D. and Warr, B. (1992) *Quality Counts: Achieving Quality in Social Care Services*,
   London: Whiting & Birch.

On registration and inspection
Davies, A. (1993) *Exploring Competence in Registration, Inspection and Quality Control*,
   London: Central Council for Education and Training in Social Work.

On total quality
Total Quality, Factsheet 29, *Personnel Management*, May 1990.

Official guidance on the relevant British Standard on quality assurance
*Guidance on the Interpretation of BS 5750: 1987 Part Two, with Reference to Social Care
   Agencies*, Social Care Agencies Sector Committee, British Quality Association, ref.
   BQA/SS Doc/1/90.

3

Planning and carrying out work with people

Preview

This chapter deals with the process of working with people. This process involves:

○ assessing needs;
○ planning and delivering, reviewing, monitoring and evaluating services.

Process of the work

The process of working with people is illustrated in the diagram below. As indicated, the sequence of activities needs to change according to circumstances. Note how the values and principles relate to, and are reflected in, all the aspects of the work. (For a definition of values and principles refer back to Chapter 1, pp. 4–5).

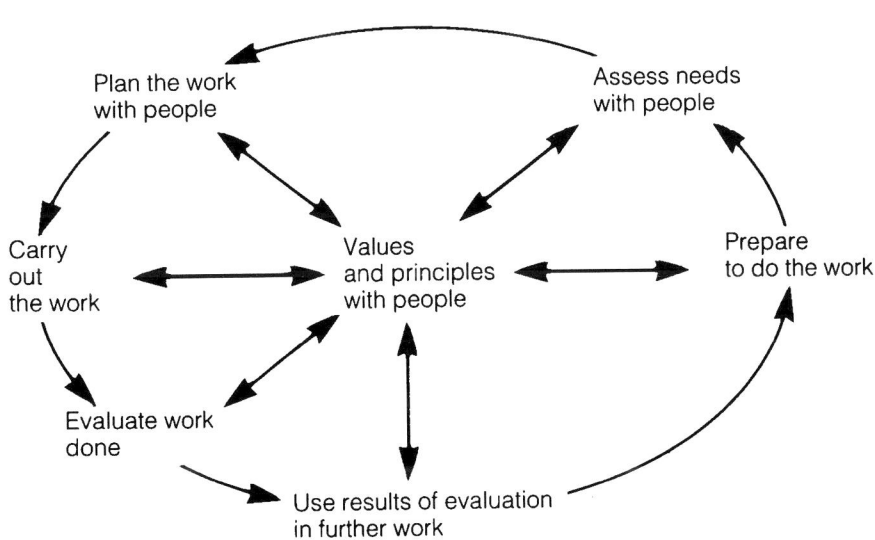

The problem with the above diagram is that in real life the sequence of work is not a series of linked, separate steps, always carried out in the same order. For example, there is a strong case for considering how the work is evaluated right at the start, rather than only at the end. Again, the objectives and the work plan may be revised in the light of experience.

Preparing to do the work

Workers have to prepare for the work about to be undertaken. An important part of this preparation is making sure they are equipped to do it, in terms of necessary resources such as time and skills.

Assessing needs with people

Assessment is the process by which workers, service users and carers identify the areas of difficulty for a person, and their needs. They then agree on a course of action in response to these.

Different views of needs

People's needs can be perceived from different standpoints. There are needs as measured against some objective standard, such as a minimum wage or dietary regime. There are also needs as people experience them. In a given situation, one person may feel completely satisfied while another has a range of needs. A person who is used to managing on a low wage may find a small bonus of enormous help in supplementing a meagre lifestyle. In contrast, to a high earner the addition of the same amount of money to a pay cheque may go unnoticed.

People's needs may be simple – for one item or service – or they may be complex – requiring a range of responses in the form of different resources and services. Their needs may be physical and practical, psychological, emotional or social.

Making an assessment

Assessment techniques may be used to gather quantitative information about people, such as their height and weight; or qualitative information, such as how they feel about walking two miles to the shops each day. Assessment involves much more than observing people. It requires the skills of getting alongside them and gaining their confidence and trust. It involves 'hands-on' experience of working with people.

There are several stages in the assessment process: the initial assessment – getting to know the person; followed by one of several levels of assessment, depending on the decision in this first stage about how complex their needs are.

Here are some key questions that may help you anticipate some of the main issues involved in making an assessment.

- How would you record your assessment?
- What issues arise for you in recording your assessment?

- How, if at all, would you involve other professionals in the process of assessing a person?
- In what specific circumstances would you always check with other professionals when making an assessment?
- How, if at all, would you take into account the rights of people when making and recording your assessment?
- How, if at all, should carers be involved in the assessment of their relatives?

Example

The following are involved in making an assessment of a person's community care needs:

- informing the person about the services available;
- the person's own assessment of their circumstances;
- the person's social, emotional, intellectual and physical development;
- the need to evaluate the assessment process with other members of the care team;
- the construction and delivery of the care plan.

Three models of assessment

Questioning model
The questioning model assumes the worker is the expert who simply asks questions to assess needs.

Procedural model
In this variant of the questioning model, the power still lies predominantly with the professionals. The worker carries out a procedure, previously laid down, for assessing the person. This procedure has little or no reference to the person's particular situation or needs. The assumption is that the managers who have drawn up the guidelines for conducting assessments know best about how the criteria should be set to match available resources to people's needs.

Exchange model
In the exchange model the service users, and their relatives, carers and friends, all have valid experiences and perceptions of the person's situation and problems. They have the right to contribute these experiences and perceptions to the assessment, on an *equal basis* with the workers, as professionals.

There are circumstances where factors such as shortage of time create pressures towards a questioning model of assessment. The exchange model should be adopted, however, wherever work *alongside* users and carers is the goal. (For more discussion of these models, read Smale *et al.* 1993, pp. 7–15.)

A whole-person assessment
Referral of a person may lead to two stages of decision making about assessment: an initial decision about what level of assessment to make, and a decision about the outcome of the assessment.

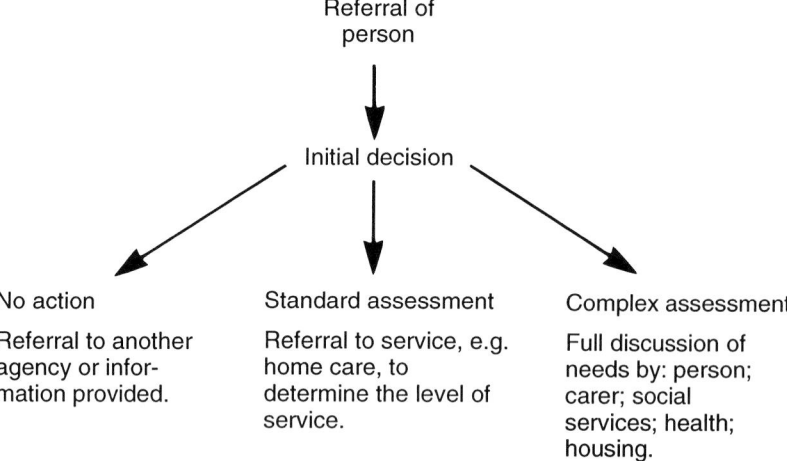

Standard assessment involves a decision to make an immediate and uncomplicated response to meeting a person's needs. Complex assessment is required where there are complications, debates and/or issues to be resolved before making decisions about providing services. Complex assessment is likely to include the following aspects:

*A*ctivity

Write down examples of two situations: one that would attract standard assessment, and one that would attract a complex assessment.

Assessment of a person should not just focus on what workers perceive as the weaknesses of that individual and base a statement of needs on that. Assessors should construct a profile of their resources and needs, including support networks and local surroundings. The assessment should be as full as is necessary to meet a person's needs, without wasting resources or being unnecessarily intrusive. It should involve the person, as potential service user, as actively as possible from the outset.

Workers should seek information first and foremost from the person about their needs and resources. This should start with the person's own account of their history, or *biography*, of how they have arrived at the present situation and what their needs are.

Bear in mind that:

- the assessment should focus on strengths (resources) as well as needs;
- the views of the person, as potential service user, are central;
- the views of any carers, and other professionals, should be sought;
- the person's perception will probably differ from that of other people, in major or minor respects;
- the more complex a person's needs are, the more information will be required and the greater the likelihood that they will need multiple services.

Every person assessed should receive:

- information at the outset, explaining what services are available;
- information after assessment, explaining the outcome of assessment and giving information about service choices open to the user and carer, any local advocacy schemes and complaints procedures.

Planning work with people

The process of care planning in community care follows fairly closely the different stages referred to here: particularly in assessment, care planning, implementation and evaluation.

In the first place, the worker should negotiate agreement with people about how their needs are to be addressed. Note that the term 'addressed' means tackled, not achieved! Nobody can guarantee to meet another person's needs.

Reaching working agreements about people's needs

Decisions should not be made in advance and then forced on people. Even where the options are limited, efforts should be made to negotiate with them and offer them real choices based on their own experiences and wishes. It is important to take into account a number of different factors, including:

- anti-oppressive practice issues;
- cultural and other differences, and equal opportunities policies;
- health and safety issues;
- any resources that will need to be developed in order to meet needs;
- the time period over which the plan will be carried out.

Let us examine an example of a group situation, where planning the work involves programming for an establishment.

*A*ctivity

Planning the work in a nursery or playgroup

Plan a five-day programme of activities for children aged 2½ to 3 years old. State how you would involve children and parents in this planning process. Complete the timetable below, using the following: sand, water, blocks, paints, dough, outside play, morning drink, lunch, afternoon drink, storytelling, rest/sleep.

	Monday	Tuesday	Wednesday	Thursday	Friday
9 am					
10 am					
11 am					
12 noon					
1 pm					
2 pm					
3 pm					
4 pm					
5 pm					

Clearly, it would have been easy to sit down on your own as a worker and simply draw up the timetable, rather like a traditional school teacher. But involving parents in the planning process raises all kinds of linked issues. These issues are to do with how far the setting has structured mechanisms for parents to participate in decision making.

The same kinds of issues come up in planning work in other areas, where individuals or groups may be involved. These include therapeutic groups, development programmes, language and speech therapy, physiotherapy, occupational therapy, hydrotherapy, foot care and acute care of patients and other people. The process of negotiating and planning is tied in with the following areas:

- how the worker prepares the setting (the work environment);
- how the worker prepares the people, in terms of discussion with them;
- how the worker supports activities such as occupational therapy;
- how the worker contributes to the planning of a programme with the user;
- how the worker deals with any anxieties that users and carers may have at the outset of a new programme or treatment.

Over and above the practical tasks of preparing users for treatment, it is important to tune into their experiences, and those of their carers, deal with any queries they have, reassure them and offer as much support as they need, without being oppressive.

Carrying out the work

Workers should ensure that the work is carried out with the fullest possible participation of the service user. This means discussing aspects of implementing the work, or changes, as they occur.

Plans should be adapted as circumstances change. For instance, the weather may improve and people who have been following an indoor programme can go outside. Conversely, a thunderstorm may suggest the need for calming activities to soothe anxious people. The aim should be to provide such activities attractively, imaginatively and in a stimulating way. The worker should use and adapt time, space, material and human resources effectively, imaginatively and safely, in indoor and outdoor environments. At the same time, people's different needs, interests, capacities and cultures need to be taken into account. It is important not to base decisions about carrying out the work on personal prejudices.

Making decisions

In all the above, workers will need to know in which areas of the work:

- they can make decisions without consulting other people;
- they must consult before making decisions;
- they must inform before making decisions;
- they must refer to another person or a group/team for a decision about how to carry out the work.

The first option is very rare, though it may arise in matters of health and safety. In all the others the list of people will probably include workers, service users and carers. The work done will need to be recorded. Recording and report writing are essential tasks at this point.

Evaluating work done

The next task is to evaluate the work done. In this process, it is important to compare the work actually done with the original goals agreed with those involved. It is also crucial to seek the views of service users and carers on the work done. Service users' evaluations must be fairly represented in the evaluations carried out by workers. Evaluations of the work by workers will need to be reported in a form that service users and carers can check against their own experience.

Using results of evaluation in further work

Evaluation is only useful if it is linked with further work. The worker needs now to feed the results of earlier evaluations into future plans. This is why the figure at the start of this chapter (p. 33) draws the process as an endless cycle of activity.

The process described here links with the process of reflective practice (see Chapter 1, p. 3) and quality assurance (see the discussion of monitoring and evaluation in Chapter 2, p. 30).

Key questions

Use these questions to check back over the material covered in the chapter and assess your grasp of it, before moving on. Discuss the questions, and responses to them, with colleagues and tutors.

○ What are the main stages in the process of carrying out work with people?
○ How would you involve users and carers in the following:
  ○ assessing their needs;
  ○ planning services with them;
  ○ providing services;
  ○ monitoring services provided;
  ○ evaluating services.
○ What are three commonly used models of assessment?
○ What main sources of information are you likely to draw on in making a complex assessment?

Relevant GNVQ/SNVQ and NVQ/SVQ Units

The material in this chapter will help with preparation for the following Health and Social Care GNVQ/SNVQ Units

Advanced Level:

  Unit 7 – Care plans

and NVQ/SVQ Units from the following National Occupational Standards

for Care:
  Key Role V – Contribute to the planning, delivery and evaluation of services which
      provide support and care
  Key Role X – Support clients during specific treatment, therapeutic and
      development programmes
for Working with Young Children:
  C.16 – Observe and assess the development and behaviour of children
  M.7 – Plan, implement and evaluate activities and experiences to promote

children's learning and development
M.8 – Plan, implement and evaluate routines for young children

Further reading

Department of Health (SSI) and Scottish Office: Social Work Services Group (1991) *Care Management and Assessment: Practitioners Guide*, London: HMSO. (This useful guide shows how the different stages of care management and planning work in practice.)

4

Creating and maintaining a person-orientated environment

Preview

This chapter deals with the work involved in maintaining a healthy, safe, secure and above all person-orientated environment. It points to key aspects with the primary purpose of benefiting people:

○ health and safety;
○ personal security;
○ the maintenance of the physical environment.

A **person-orientated** approach to work with people involves an element of deliberate risk taking. It involves giving people the right to a proper degree of choice, if their quality of life is to be maximized, whether in hospital, in other areas of residential and daycare, or in their own homes.

Institutions are for people, not people for institutions

There is more to productive and fulfilling work with people than simply keeping them safe and meeting their basic needs for warmth, feeding and rest. Any facility, organization, day centre, hospital, or residential setting dealing with people in the human services has three main goals:

1 custody – keeping control over the people it houses;
2 maintenance – keeping people housed and fed;
3 benefit to people – meeting people's needs.

Research indicates that custodial establishments tend to carry on regardless with the first two of these functions, while the third one tends to be rather precarious (see Street *et al.* 1966). Activities benefiting people are not only discarded in crises. They can be abandoned for all sorts of reasons, at any time. Although guaranteeing people's health, safety and quality of life – that is, the *custody* and *maintenance* activities – is the priority, these activities should not take over and largely or entirely replace the *benefit to people* activities.

A*ctivity*

Choose any work setting you know well. Jot down under the three headings – Custody, Maintenance and Benefit to people – an example of how each of these goals should be met in that setting.

Discuss with colleagues your views about whether *benefit to people* is achieved as well as it might be.

Ask yourself whether *benefit to people* loses out to *custody* and/or *maintenance*.

Maintaining a person-orientated environment

What makes a residential or daycare establishment feel like home? When does a residential or nursing home provide a domestic rather than an institutional environment? These are very difficult questions to answer precisely. We all know by the feel of a situation whether it appeals to us when we go into it, but on what is that intuition based? Are there some criteria that we can use to make judgements about our own work situation and those of other people?

A good deal of research has been done over the years into the regimes of different day and residential settings where children and adults, especially older people, live. A particularly useful piece of research was carried out on the regime of remand prisons (King and Morgan 1976, pp. 41–2). It produced a simple checklist, readily transferable to other human services. This lists aspects, under the following headings, as particularly contributing to the regime and, therefore, to the quality of the living environment: block treatment, rigidity, restrictiveness, supervision and autonomy.

Block treatment

Block treatment refers to the extent to which residents, patients or service users are treated in a regimented way about when they get up, eat meals, wash, have baths and so on.

Rigidity

Rigidity refers to whether or not people have to carry out particular activities at defined times. Do people have the choice of staying in bed and eating later, or washing and bathing when they choose? Can they have privacy in their room? For example, can they entertain a visitor instead of having to wait while their room is cleaned at a particular time each day, regardless of what they are doing? Are lights switched off at a fixed time? Are the outside doors locked after a certain time?

Restrictiveness

Restrictiveness refers to the extent to which the service user has access to all parts of the establishment, or is denied access to some of them. How much choice do people have over where and how they meet their visitors and eat their meals? Can they take food to their rooms? Can they prepare food and hot and cold drinks in their rooms? Can people choose whether they share a room with other people? For example, has a person who has been a cook throughout their life the right to go into the kitchen and make use of the facilities to prepare a snack or a meal? There may be a tension between health and safety regulations and the goal of maximizing the independence and quality of life of the service user. For example, in one local authority no resident can be in a kitchen unless the staff all put on white coats.

Supervision

How far do people have the right to privacy and how much are they subject to surveillance – being watched, throughout the day and the night? Are they watched throughout their leisure time? Do staff watch them rather than join in playing games with them, for example? Do staff watch the residents through glass screens, one-way mirrors or peepholes in doors, without them knowing when, and by whom, they are being watched?

Autonomy

There are two components of autonomy: self-responsibility and collective responsibility. Self-responsibility refers to how far people have choice and control over their immediate personal activities. For example, can they wear the clothes they choose? How much control do they have over the washing of their clothes? Can they control the switching on and off of radios, televisions and lights in the various living areas, including the rooms where they sleep? Can people choose with whom they share a room, either the room they live in or the daytime communal living areas?

Collective responsibility concerns the extent to which people as a group have control over, and can take part in, various group activities, such as organizing meetings, holding whist drives and various other social, leisure or sporting occasions.

One of the most interesting features of the application of the above list to a particular work setting is how often staff tend to rule out specific items as being irrelevant or impracticable, on the grounds that health and safety, the protection of the person, or staff shortages would make changes impossible.

*E*xample

Day or residential care

Here are some indicators of institutionally based and person-based programmes.

Institutionally based (meeting service needs)	Person based (meeting individual needs)
staff eat separately from service users/residents	service users/residents and staff eat where they choose
residents/users have no choice about the timing or menu of meals and how they are served (e.g. cafeteria)	residents/users can choose the timing menu, and manner of serving meals

A*ctivity*

Think about the major differences between institutionally based and person-based programmes. Answer the following questions.

1 Is your work setting institutionally based or person based?
2 Can you think of any other ways of distinguishing between institutionally based and person-based programmes, in any setting?
3 What advantages and disadvantages of each approach can you identify?
4 How would you attempt to shift from, say, an institutionally based to a person-based approach? What difficulties might you come across? How would you tackle these?

It will help if you can discuss your response to these tasks with colleagues, fellow learners and assessors.

Work with babies and young children

The ideas about insitutionally based and person-based programmes also apply to work with babies and young children. The physical setting for work with, and care of, babies and young children should be warm, safe, healthy and hygienic. Above all, however, the staff, parents and other helpers should be working to maximize the quality of life of everyone in the situation.

The nursery or playgroup should be homely, attractive and inviting. It should provide a variety of stimulating activities, as well as opportunities for relaxation, rest and sleep. It should be a place where excitement and noise can be part of play and self-expression, as well as quietness and reflectiveness. These activities may go on at different times or simultaneously. It may not be easy to reconcile the different phases at which children of varying ages become active or need rest and sleep. The task of maintaining the day-to-day programme of nursery catering, say, for babies aged 9 months through to children aged 5, is very demanding. It requires sensitive work with individuals, as well as careful planning of, and work with and within, larger groups of children and adults.

Workers are responsible for ensuring that the setting is geared to meeting the needs of babies and young children rather than the babies and young children being adjusted to meet the needs of the setting. Ask yourself how far a setting is child-orientated. The table on the following page sets out some indicators.

Try adding more items to the list, as they occur to you.

Maintaining a safe environment

The idea that a person in a residential or daycare setting will be safer than at home simply by being there, is a fallacy. People are only as safe as the foresight of staff allows them to be.

Child-orientated	Setting-orientated
The workers play on tables and on the floor with the children.	The workers chat in a corner or round desks at the front and observe the children playing.
The workers allow children to paint and cut out paper shapes, as they wish.	The workers give the children ready-cut shapes and guide them in colouring them in. They remove the activity from the tables and floor at the precise time the activity is programmed to stop.
The workers help the children stick their own work onto the wallboards.	The workers put on the walls the children's work they select as suitable.
The workers sometimes prepare food with the children.	The workers always prepare all food separately.
The workers eat with the children.	The workers eat separately.

Hazards to safety

The following are some examples of hazards in a person's own home, but the list could be much longer:

- pans on the kitchen stove, with hot liquid in them;
- unguarded stairs;
- unguarded cupboards containing toxic substances;
- electric sockets;
- sharp surfaces;
- iron on the ironing board, plugged in;
- implements (knives, scissors), left within reach.

Here is a list of the kinds of risks to safety that an older person could encounter in a domestic environment away from home:

- unfamiliarity with the location of emergency fire exits;
- corridors which are difficult to negotiate with a zimmer frame;
- steps and uneven floors which make wheelchairs difficult to manoeuvre unaided;
- fire extinguishers missing, hidden or inaccessible;
- tables and chairs which clutter up passages and other busy areas;
- leads from electric floor polishers and vacuum cleaners left trailing over the floors;
- tool boxes and dust sheets that repair workers and decorators have left lying around.

Relevant legislation and regulations

The Health and Safety at Work etc. Act 1974 covers the steps an employer should take to maintain a safe, accident-free working environment. This Act requires employers to ensure that all premises are safe and free of risks to the health of employees, and other people using their premises (Part 1, Sections 2–9). It set up the Health and Safety Commission and the Health and Safety

Executive. These bodies oversee the proper implementation of the Act and ensure that any abuses of it are investigated (Part 1, Sections 10–14). The Health and Safety Commission has issued an Approved Code of Practice entitled *Management of Health and Safety at Work*. This gives guidance on how to use the Management of Health and Safety at Work Regulations 1992 in all the work settings they cover (Health and Safety Commission 1992). All employees working with people have responsibilities under the Health and Safety at Work etc. Act 1974 and the Approved Code of Practice to ensure their own health and safety, and that of other workers and service users and carers on the premises.

Some sections of the Environmental Protection Act 1990 are particularly relevant to work with people. Much work with people involves manual work. According to the Health and Safety Executive, manual handling accounts for 34 per cent of all accidents at work that cause injuries (Health and Safety Executive 1992).

The Manual Handling Operations Regulations 1992 contains a useful checklist to apply to a particular work setting. This covers factors to which the employer must have regard, for example, when assessing tasks, loads, working environments and workers' individual capabilities, and when determining whether protective clothing hinders movement.

Maintaining a healthy environment

Cleanliness goes hand in hand with the prevention of infections in a living and working environment.

Preventing infections
The following are typical questions used as a self-check by workers, in maintaining a clean environment.

- Are there signs of dust, dirt, mud, scum, faeces, grease or vomit anywhere in the living and working environment?
- Are the key areas for cooking, washing, toileting, feeding and resting cleaned frequently enough to remove the risks of infection?
- Are different methods of cleaning – dusting, vacuuming, wiping, washing with soap and water, disinfecting, fumigating – used appropriately and frequently enough?

Relevant regulations
The Control of Substances Hazardous to Health Regulations 1988 deal with the circumstances and the manner in which dangerous substances should be used.

Maintaining children's safety

*ctivity*

Make a list of the hazards that children may encounter in a domestic environment.

The young child is particularly vulnerable to accidents, injuries and illnesses. The environment where young children play, eat and sleep must be kept clean and the risk of accidents minimized. Equipment that presents no danger to adults can have sharp corners that are hazardous to a running or falling child. Bleaches and other dangerous substances should be secured in cupboards with child-safety catches. All bottles, jars, etc., containing dangerous substances should have child-resistant tops.

Relationship between home environment and care/education environment

A*ctivity*

List the preparations you would make to ensure that young children are safe when staff in a nursery take them on an outing.

Measures to ensure the safety of children on outings normally will include:

- making adequate preparations;
- checking insurance is adequate;
- checking while out what each child is doing;
- ensuring that an adult is close by all children at all times;
- ensuring parents who wish to contribute and participate can do so;
- informing other parents fully, before and after the event;
- minimizing hazards to children from the environment, such as traffic, pollution, strangers, animals, poisons and water.

Maintaining privacy, dignity and personal hygiene

Managing risks

There is no way to remove all the risks associated with the caring environment without seriously violating people's privacy and undermining their freedom to choose, plan and act independently.

A*ctivity*

List the arguments for and against taking away the pills of a woman arriving in residential care, who until now has been administering them to herself satisfactorily.

There is a tension between allowing people freedom to control their own medication and the responsibility staff may feel for residents' health and safety. On one hand, a person who is used to administering their own pills is likely to feel more in control of the situation and more respected as a trustworthy person if they can continue to do so. On the other hand, the staff may feel vulnerable to criticism, and possible disciplinary action, if that person makes a mistake and their health suffers as a result. This raises the question of how far managers support staff in taking reasonable risks in order to maximize the quality of life of residents.

Respecting people's dignity

There is also a tension between ensuring the cleanliness and safety of the physical environment for residents and service users, and caring for and treating each person as an individual, with dignity. (This relates to the principles discussed in Chapter 1.)

Some establishments have buildings or regimes that do not allow people to be respected. It can be humiliating to have to undress in your room, put on a dressing gown that is too small, or in any case not your own, and walk down a corridor, past staff, other residents and visitors, to the bathroom.

In how many residential and daycare establishments do staff feel confident about approaching service users and asking them quietly if they want to have a private word about help with incontinence? Possibly this could involve using advice and support from the incontinence adviser on their next visit.

Staff need to work in a way that maximizes the self-respect and privacy of residents. In a residential home for older people, one of the care assistants was in the habit of standing in the dining room after the meal and calling out 'hands up if you want a wee!' This may make the work of staff quicker, but hardly treats residents with respect.

Tension between maintaining privacy and addressing loneliness

*A*ctivity

Ask yourself and colleagues these questions about a residential establishment known to you and/or them.

- Can people live by choice in a single room in the residential establishment?
- Do they have a real choice about whether they share a room with somebody else?
- Can residents who want to share a room choose the person with whom they share it?
- Do staff routinely come into a resident's room without knocking first and asking if it's all right to enter?

These questions point to choices, which staff should normally discuss with residents, rather than decide without reference to them. One aspect to be borne in mind is that many older and/or housebound people, especially those who live alone, lack physical contact with other people. Many people lack opportunities to express their sexuality in such situations. Ways need to be found to ensure that residential accommodation, including nursing homes, is similar to, say, hotel accommodation. It should be normal for residents to live as independently as possible, and that includes developing relationships, which may be sexual, with each other.

Maximizing the quality of life involves taking risks

Some people take excessive precautions in situations where the risk is minimal. There may be conflicts of interest between procedures and people's needs. Although it is necessary to comply with relevant legislation, the principles of good hygiene, health and safety at work should be balanced against giving people the maximum independence in their living environment. For example, an elderly man who has had a stroke may be at risk if he returns after the stroke to live alone in his own home. But workers may consider the level of risk to be acceptable, in the interest of maximizing his independence, provided he carries an alarm to summon help in an emergency. In such a situation, assessment of people's circumstances should lead to sufficient resources and support being provided to minimize risks, while enabling them to retain their autonomy.

Assessing people at risk

What does 'at risk' mean? It is a term used to describe people considered to be vulnerable, because of some particular aspect of their circumstances. For example, the following are at risk, in different ways:

- babies and young children;
- older, frail people;
- older people living alone;
- children and young people who are orphaned or refugees.

It is important to note, however, that within these categories there are many people who manage their lives perfectly well and are not at risk. We should guard against assuming that someone is vulnerable just because they are old, or that a child is vulnerable just because they have no birth parents. General procedures for assessing, planning and carrying out care plans for adults at risk should follow the same general sequence as those for children.

The fact that someone is elderly and frail, or elderly and living alone, does not necessarily mean that the care worker should be seeking to persuade them to move into residential accommodation. If a person is frail, the criteria used to determine their needs should include how much and what kinds of help and support are required to enable that person to live as independent and full a life as possible. The following are key areas to include.

- Does the person need help, and if so what kinds of help, to get about (e.g. zimmer frame, walking stick)?
- Does the person need help with getting in and out of the bath?
- Does the person need help with cooking meals?

If an older person is living alone, the above questions may be added to, as follows.

- Does the person live alone from choice or through other circumstances?

- Does the person need support in order to continue living safely in the same accommodation? If so, what kinds of community resource does the person need?

It may help to distinguish between:

- a high-risk situation – where a person is unable to cope with daily functions such as eating and getting about, at all;
- a medium-risk situation – where a person can cope with some daily help with key tasks such as cooking;
- a low-risk situation – where a person does not need help more than once a week, for example with cleaning, to maintain the quality of life.

Key questions

Use these questions to check back over the material covered in the chapter and assess your grasp of it, before moving on. Discuss the questions, and responses to them, with colleagues and tutors.

○ Apart from block treatment, what ingredients contribute to a custodial regime?
○ What are the key indicators that a playgroup or nursery is setting-orientated rather than child-orientated?
○ What measures will need to be taken to ensure the safety of children on an outing?
○ What hazards are typical of the following situations:
  ○ an older person at home;
  ○ a child at home?
○ What illustrations can you give of a person being:
  ○ high risk;
  ○ medium risk;
  ○ low risk?

Relevant GNVQ/SNVQ and NVQ/SVQ Units

The material in this chapter will help with preparation for the following Health and Social Care GNVQ/SNVQ Units

Advanced Level:
  Unit 5 – Health promotion

and NVQ/SVQ Units from the following National Occupational Standards

for Care:
  Key Role U – Contribute to the maintenance of an environment for effective care
  Key Role V – Contribute to the planning, delivery and evaluation of services which
      provide support and care
for Working with Young Children:
  C.8 – Set out and clear away play activities
  E.1 – Maintain a child oriented environment
  E.2 – Maintain the safety of children

Further reading

Information on health and hygiene in the living and working environment is available from the Health Education Authority, Health Education Board for Scotland, Health Promotion Authority for Wales and the Health Research Board for Ireland.

For material on health and safety, you will find the local offices and the library of the Health and Safety Executive are useful sources of help. The library's address is at the end of this book.

Department of Health, Social Services Inspectorate (1991) *Homes are for Living in*, London: HMSO.

Houghton, D. and McColgan, M. (forthcoming) *Working with Children*, London: Collins Educational.

Social Services Inspectorate (1993) *Evaluating Performance in Child Protection*, London: HMSO.

5

Enabling people to develop and live to their full potential

Preview

Work with people requires sensitivity to the individual and an awareness of how people are perceived, labelled and dealt with as they move through their lives. For instance, workers need to avoid viewing young children simply as dependants who are potentially disruptive. In the same way they need to avoid viewing older people as dependants who are potentially a burden on everyone with whom they come into contact. This chapter uses the idea of personhood to put these issues into a wider perspective. It discusses:

○ how to enable people of all ages to develop and live to their maximum potential;
○ the key issues that are raised by this task.

When do people reach their full potential?

Here are two common statements, made about people at different stages of their lives.

- 'Once people reach the age of 50, they are over the hill and not worth employing.'
- 'Children are basically savages. Growing up involves civilizing them.'

Statements like this are frequently made. They illustrate prejudices rather than being based on facts about growing up or ageing. People can achieve their full potential at any age. These statements are reminders of how difficult it is to rid ourselves of particular theories and assumptions about how people grow up, develop, mature, decay and eventually, if not prematurely, die. We have been brought up with these assumptions, probably without even being aware of many of them. Work with people demands the ability to stand back from these beliefs and view them critically. It also requires the worker to value people as they are, as people, with all their differences. Here is an activity that enables you to explore how much value you attach to different people.

A *ctivity*

You are a property owner with eight single rooms to let. You acquire eight tenants: a healthy working nurse, a building contractor, a homosexual person, a black person, an old person, an HIV-positive person, an obese person and a blind person. However, a good friend becomes homeless and you agree to let them have a room. You have to give one of your tenants notice to quit. Whom do you choose?

Some time later, the same thing happens to another good friend. To whom do you next give notice?

Repeat the process until there are no rooms left.

Discuss your list with other people. Get them to carry out the activity and compare results.

Note that this activity is very powerful. It can raise very strong emotions, in you and in other people. You need to have space to talk afterwards about how you have tackled it.

The above activity is about valuing people as persons. It tends to show that we all have ideas about which categories of people we value more or less than other categories of people. These ideas may be hidden in everyday life, but are likely to be expressed, sometimes directly but more likely indirectly, in our work with people. Clearly, what is needed is a perspective that encourages anti-oppressive work with people. It should challenge prejudices and assumptions about people's differences (see Chapter 1, pp. 7–9, for a discussion of what is involved in anti-oppressive work).

Valuing people throughout their lives: the idea of personhood

We shall use the idea of personhood to help examine how to work positively with people, throughout their lives.

Personhood is the confirmation that a particular individual has a socially significant identity. Unfortunately, you cannot simply develop your own personhood. It depends largely on how other people treat you. Bearing this in mind, if you achieve full personhood at your age and in your particular circumstances, you can expect:

- to be regarded as a valid individual in your own right;
- to have the kind of rights and choices appropriate for someone of your age and needs;
- to be respected equally with other people, irrespective of individual differences, such as ethnicity, gender, social class and so on.

Comparing experiences at different times and places in people's lives

It is useful to compare and contrast, as Roger Clough does (Clough 1981, p. 157), the experiences of residential work with children, living and being educated in a community home, and older people.

Comparisons
In the two settings, the custody and maintenance functions (see Chapter 4, p. 42, for a discussion of these) are similar. For example, staff are likely to experience similar pressures about monitoring where people in their charge are, and ensuring they get up, dress, wash, feed and go to bed.

Contrasts
First, in the older people's home, the staff are younger and fitter than the people with whom they are working. Both staff and residents tend to agree that the basic purpose of the setting is to care for residents, though they do not always agree on how this should be achieved.

Second, while the child is dependent on staff for 'good reports, good teaching and humane treatment', the old person is dependent on services to meet their physical needs (Clough 1981, p. 157).

Third, 'while both groups are aware of the effect of their behaviour on the staff, the old are probably more prepared to modify behaviour to help staff' (Clough 1981, p. 157).

Finally, staff are trying to socialize the children, or enable them to relate to other people. That task is not central to work with the older people.

The situation is very complex. As people grow older, their circumstances and needs stay the same in some respects but change in others.

Different nurturing practices

People's circumstances are defined by the society in which they are located. This is illustrated by the great variety of practices affecting both the rearing of children and caring for older people. You can test this out by discussing and comparing personal experiences with colleagues and friends who have been brought up in different cultures and countries.

Valuing and working with people's differences

Throughout their lives people change – and react to change – physically, emotionally and socially. Though a progressive development is usually associated with children and young people growing up, and decay with the ageing of older people, in reality people experience these positive and negative features through the course of their lives. For example, it is very important when working with older people not to reinforce the stereotype of old age as being the last, decaying stage through which largely useless people go before they die. Unfortunately, many older people experience the negative effects of being treated in a way that reinforces this sort of stereotype..

Differences through the life course
Consider differences throughout people's lives. The list of key moments or phases in a person's life is unique to each situation. Here is a list of some of the main significant points in the life of a person in a Western industrial society:

- birth;
- first day at school;

- puberty (first period/first shave);
- first boyfriend/girlfriend;
- first job;
- wedding;
- setting up first home;
- buying a house;
- moving house;
- break-up of relationship;
- death of close relative;
- birth of child;
- an accident;
- menopause;
- birth of first grandchild;
- hospital;
- redundancy;
- retirement.

It would be useful to use personal experience, or that of a service user, carer, colleague or friend, to make a list of the significant points in the life of a person from a different society. We can make the following general points.

- People develop, change and age at different rates. At each stage, their needs change. Their needs range from physical, to psychological, to social aspects of development.
- People's differences, and cultural differences in their situation, will affect the rate and nature of the changes and transitions they undergo. In work with them, their community language and culture should be valued.
- The societal and cultural context in which people live their lives will contribute to shaping the kinds of key moments they identify as being significant. Other factors contributing to this shaping process include factors such as people's gender, age and class.

Supporting people in developing their personhood involves maximizing the benefit they can gain from relationships with other people.
  Relationships involve enabling people to:

- keep in touch and interact with other people – this includes dealing with difficulties in relationships;
- be adequate as relatives – this includes being a good mother, father, sister, brother, son or daughter.

(See Chapter 1, pp. 19–25, for a discussion of the development and management of positive working relationships with people.)
  The next part of this chapter deals with some key issues that are likely to arise in work with three groups: children, disabled adults and older people. We shall start with young children.

Enabling babies, children and young people to develop their personhood

Working with babies and young children

Babies and young children develop at different rates. Often, their domestic environments are part of a multi-cultural society. Workers need to celebrate and build on these differences and not see them as problems.

The physical care of babies and children affects their emotional development. Babies need a secure, anxiety-free, unhurried feed as much as older children may need an understanding tolerance of their argumentative approach to day-to-day interaction with adults.

Promotion of the development of babies

The growth and development, including language learning, of babies are fostered by making sure their needs for physical care, adequate nutrition and appropriate stimulation are met. The development patterns of babies vary widely in different cultures. Therefore, it is wise to be wary of imposing rules about stages of development based on one particular culture or set of experiences.

Whilst adequate sleep is essential to health and development, the sleep patterns of babies and young children vary as widely as those of adults.

Physical development of children

Most babies and young children develop rapidly. During infancy and childhood they are likely to develop in even faster spurts, at certain periods. Workers need to match the setting for care, plan and rest to the varying developmental and special needs of babies and young children.

Emotional, intellectual and social development

Sound intellectual development depends on adequate stimulation in a secure physical setting. Social development depends on progressive experience of supportive interaction, first with parents and later with other adults.

The diversity of patterns of child-rearing and children's needs makes it necessary for the worker to make their personal experience the basis of work with children in general. One way of counteracting this is to involve parents, relatives and friends as much as possible in work with babies and children. These significant adults play vital roles in children's development. Where mothers work, for example, fathers, grandparents and older sisters and brothers often can nurture infants and children in their place.

Children's social and emotional development depends largely on the quality of their relationships and interaction with adults and other children. As children grow older, they may be encouraged to cooperate more in their play with each other. As children interact, they will inevitably come into competition, and even conflict with each other.

Ways of encouraging children to resolve their conflicts amicably include:

- mediating;
- intervening to prevent physical confrontations;
- diverting the attention of one or more children.

Attention spans of young children

Young children often flit from activity to activity every few minutes. The attention of a young child can be easily distracted from, say, picking up bricks to the jigsaw puzzle a nearby child is holding. Young children learn through touching, feeling, smelling and putting things in their mouths, encouraging curiosity.

It is important to exclude from the play area any small items such as beads, or sharp surfaces that could cause injuries. At the same time, children's curiosity is healthy. Even though the toddler who constantly struggles to reach every new toy that catches their eye is more at risk of falling, adults should encourage this sort of curiosity.

Encouraging children's self-awareness and ability to communicate

It is important to make opportunities that encourage children to take the initiative in communicating. The qualities of self-reliance and independence are desirable, and work done with children should reinforce these.

Play

Play is one important way in which young children learn and develop. Play has an impact on every aspect of a child's life: physical, intellectual, emotional, cultural and social. The benefits in these aspects are closely linked.

There are different kinds of play: imaginative, physical, constructive and creative. Children may play with blocks, sand, water, dough and paints. In fact, almost all aspects of work with babies and young children can involve play. Babies can be tickled gently while their nappies are being changed. Older children can clear away small toys at the end of the day, as a game.

Storytelling and books

Storytelling is an activity that requires a relatively quiet place where children can sit round. Sometimes they will enjoy the physical closeness of sitting next to, or on the lap of, the adult storyteller or other adult listeners. The images and words used in books should be non-discriminatory. The choice of books in the workplace should be carefully monitored and matched as far as possible to the diversity of young children and adults using the setting.

Books provide pleasure and stimulation through their physical appearance. There is pleasure, for example, in picking a book up, turning its pages and discovering a particularly well-loved illustration. There is also pleasure in listening to someone reading from a book. Storytelling is a highly valued part of the adult culture of many societies. In many societies adults often enjoy being told stories as much as children.

New books can be a major source of stimulation for children. The repetition of familiar incidents in a well-loved story is reassuring and, like a pantomime, an occasion for the listeners to take part in the storytelling along with the reader. It is hard to avoid much-used books becoming tattered, but it is worth bearing in mind that the newer the appearance of a book the easier it is to persuade children to value and preserve it.

Nursery rhymes and songs

Traditional rhymes and poems, sung or recited by children, are important sources of learning. Children can get a lot of pleasure from the repetition of their favourite rhymes. These will vary greatly according to the culture of the children. Different rhymes and songs will often emerge from adults as well as children taking part in everyday activities. Particular cultural events and festivals will often be celebrated in the work setting.

Using a book corner
A quiet, well-lit, warm place that is accessible to children, with new-looking, clean, attractively illustrated books, can provide a haven for them. It can be an escape from more boisterous activity and an opportunity for them to explore the pleasures of books for themselves in their own time, at their own pace.

Working with children and young people

It is commonly argued that in work with children and young people a balance needs to be struck between care and control. On one hand, they need nurturing and supporting; on the other hand, they need clear limits to what is acceptable behaviour, and disciplining when they go beyond them.

Two common difficulties in the control of children and young people arise:

- when adults are not able to set clear, consistent boundaries round what are acceptable activities;
- when adults leave themselves too little room to manoeuvre when dealing with the possibility of the boundaries being overstepped.

A*ctivity*

Consider this extract from a conversation between a care worker and a child aged 8 in residential care. Choose from the four options listed the most appropriate response by the worker, to complete the extract.

Worker: Don't switch the TV on. It's too late to start watching it now.
Child: I'll do what I like.
Worker: I told you not to.
Child: Just try and stop me.
Worker: . . .

    (a)   'If you switch that TV on, I'll put a brick through it.'
    (b)   'If you switch that TV on, I'll tell Mr K to punish you.'
    (c)   'If you switch that TV on, I shall be very cross.'
    (d)   (Worker says nothing and walks away.)

Here are some comments on each of the above options.

(a) This option is the least desirable, offering the worker's aggression in exchange for the opposition of the child.
(b) This option refers the problem to another person.
(c) This shows the child that the worker has authority, will react, yet keeps the worker's options open on how to handle the next response of the child. The key is for the worker not to back themselves into a corner from which

only one response is possible. In that situation, the child may test the worker's ability to make that response.

(d) It is undesirable for the worker to opt out in this way.

Impairment, disability and personhood

Meeting children's different needs

Approximately one-fifth of children are likely to need special educational provision at some point in their schooling. It is important that special needs provision is made on the basis of children's needs and is not regarded as a response to their personal inadequacies. It is preferable to think of children's special needs as arising from the fact that all children, like all adults, are different. Some of these differences produce different needs for services and resources, to enable children to reach their full potential.

The different terms used to describe special needs should be noted carefully. **Learning difficulties** are what used to be called 'mental handicap', an expression now regarded as a negative description, or label, of people. The term **learning difference** may be used in place of learning difficulties. While children can inherit conditions making them more prone to learning difficulties, these difficulties can be increased by other features of children's backgrounds and environments. Down's syndrome is the commonest condition associated with learning difficulties.

Disability and sensory impairment

Whereas impairment describes a medical condition, disability is the term used to induce the circumstances in which a person is oppressed through being defined as disabled. (See Chapter 1, p. 9, for a discussion of these terms.)

*E*xample

Consider two children, both with a similar degree of congenital visual impairment. Child A remains impaired, is given appropriate support and reassurance from a specialist worker, uses high technology equipment and Braille. Child B is labelled as having needs that can only be met in a residential school. Child A goes on to acquire a range of self-care skills in mobility and daily living. Child A then goes into higher education and pursues a full-time professional career. Child B is provided with no specialist help and any lack of educational progress is put down to 'being blind'. Child B shows how disability is a socially constructed definition that oppresses a person and is a separate matter from the physical impairment.

Community care for disabled people

Many able-bodied people will have undergone tests and examinations relating to impairments. But they won't have been defined as disabled people, and so won't have been excluded from mainstream activities in society on the grounds of disability. For example, a man breaks his leg and injures his back playing professional football and goes on to become a manager of a football club. Another man with a similar injury, sustained in a factory, recovers full mobility but is assessed as an invalid and excluded from the workplace on the grounds of his disability.

How can the worker empower a disabled person who is a potential user of community care services?

There are several key stages:

- listen to what the disabled person is saying;
- discuss with the person the agency view and/or the professional view of their problem;
- use the views of the person, the worker and the agency as the basis for negotiating a care plan with the person.

Types of impairment	Examples of symptoms
Physical	Being unable to bend down Finding it hard to wash and dress Not being able to have a bath Finding it impossible to go to the toilet unaided
Sensory	Deafness or partial hearing Being unable to smell, touch or taste Being blind or partially sighted
Mental	Being unable to reason clearly Finding it difficult to remember things
Emotional	Finding it hard to relax with people Being too anxious or stressed to develop positive relationships with people Finding it difficult to exchange emotions Finding demonstrations of affection or intimacy impossible

The examples in the above table may vary from very minor to very major impairments. The worker needs to give the person with an impairment enough information to enable them to decide what sort of help is needed.

Older people and personhood

Work in the residential setting

All too often, the daytime visitor to a residential home for older people will be confronted with a lounge, either with rows of chairs, or a circle of chairs all ranged round the edge of the room. A television may be switched on at one end of the room. The visitor asking why there are no other activities going on may be told that the residents don't want them. Many smaller residential homes do not have two lounges to enable different activities to take place. In the larger homes, however, where there may be a whole range of rooms available, the issue is whether the staff and the residents believe that someone's life has to be over, and personhood surrendered, when they go into a home. Clearly, this is unacceptable.

Would residential work with older people be improved or harmed if it was viewed as part of the housing and leisure sectors, rather than linked with the health and social services? Many older people resent being labelled as sick and useless, simply because they are old. We could follow through the principle of providing a choice of caring and supporting services for people to maximize the quality of their lives, under the NHS and Community Care Act 1990. In such circumstances, the residential home could become much more like a hotel than a hospital. Of course, nursing, chiropody, social work and other services would be available as and when required, but simply on the same basis as other 'hotel services'.

The worker needs to start from the assumption that an older person has the same right to personhood as someone at any other stage of life. This means that the residential setting should be able to offer a full range of activities for older people. One problem, of course, is that the pressure on homes to provide cost-effective services that compete with other facilities may make it more difficult to keep a range of activities going. Often, however, residents themselves and their friends, carers, visitors and volunteers – including school students – form a rich resource for the generation of activities. These may include music, dancing (for seated as well as mobile residents), reminiscence and other activities enabling people to maintain social and sexual relation-ships. **Reminiscence work** with people involves enabling them to recall their experiences, perhaps using stimulus materials and interpersonal or group dis-cussion.

At a more personal level, older people need the same facilities to enable them to maintain relationships as any other people. For example, there is a case for providing a double bed in every single room of an older person's home. This would enable older people who want to continue to engage in intimate relationships with other people to do so without having to request special accommodation.

The following list depicts the process of work with a person, to provide them with community care:

1 assessment with the person;
2 setting up the criteria for assuring quality of care;
3 planning care with the person;
4 delivering a package of care to the person.

Care for the person may be provided in a variety of ways: for example, through residential provision, through daycare support in the person's own home, or through a combination of these. While most of the people needing community care are older, and a good proportion are over 70, younger people may need support as well. For example, the parents who are unable to cope with all the demands of their young children might need help, and so might the young person with HIV/AIDS.

A range of carers for older people may exist. They are likely to include friends, relatives and neighbours. The tasks they are likely to share with the community care worker include financial management, cleaning, washing, bathing, dressing and undressing, shopping and ironing.

Drawing threads together: working with people throughout their lives

We have explored some common themes throughout the life course and some themes characteristic of work with people at different ages. Now we shall bring into the discussion aspects of inequality that contribute to the principles of anti-oppressive practice described in Chapter 1 (pp. 3, 7–9).

A comparison of childhood, adulthood, disability and old age in Western industrialized societies suggests a difference that is vital to anti-oppressive work with people. Consider the following table:

	Dependence	*Independence*
Children Working adults Disabled people Older people	Yes Yes Yes	Yes

This indicates that in an important sense children, disabled people and older people tend to experience, and to be limited by, aspects of their dependence on other people. Speaking generally, it is working adults who are most likely to experience independence in society. Now compare the following table with the one above:

	Moving towards greater dependence	*Moving away from dependence*
Children Disabled people Older people	 Yes Yes	Yes

A person's circumstances may be affected further by their gender and social class. For example, in some countries politicians and members of royal families seem to gain in status, by virtue of age alone, as they get older. Unskilled workers, in contrast, are compulsorily retired at a fixed age.

*A*ctivity

Try to think of at least one exception – in the past or in the present, in your own experience or in a film or book – to the general categorization of children, disabled people and older people as dependent.

Here are some examples:

- deaf musician or composer;
- disabled athlete;
- child Emperor;
- child prodigy;
- venerated old prophet.

Each example illustrates how an exception to the general category of dependence can be found, where some particular aspect of privilege or power intervenes to counteract the inequality.

What is significant is not the existence of an exception such as Stephen Hawking, the brilliant, virtually immobilized scientist, to disprove the rule. Rather, it is significant that most people are stuck in their dependent situation. They have no prospect of being able to draw on some extraordinary factor, like the above examples, to liberate themselves.

Work with children, disabled people and older people needs to:

- enable them to achieve and maintain personhood;
- enable them to transcend their dependence;
- counteract the oppressive features of their situation.

Key questions

Use these questions to check back over the material covered in the chapter and assess your grasp of it, before moving on. Discuss the questions, and responses to them, with colleagues and tutors.

- O Can you think of some points of comparison and contrast between the experiences of those who work with older people and those who work with younger people in the residential setting?
- O What is personhood?
- O What measures would you take to try to maintain the personhood of:
  - o a baby;
  - o a young child;
  - o a person with a learning difference;
  - o an older person?

Relevant GNVQ/SNVQ and NVQ/SVQ Units

The material in this chapter will help with preparation for the following Health and Social Care GNVQ/SNVQ Units

Advanced Level:
    Unit 4 – Psychological and social aspects of health and social care
    and NVQ Units from the following National Occupational Standards
for Care:
    Key role W – Support the maintenance and development of client identity and
        relationships
for Working with Young Children:
    C.4 – Support for children's social and emotional development
    C.5 – Promote children's social and emotional development
    C.6 – Contribute to the management of children's behaviour
    C.7 – Provide for the management of children's behaviour
    C.9 – Work with young children

Further reading

For background on the idea of personhood
Hockey, J. and James, A. (1993) *Growing Up and Growing Old: Ageing and Dependency in the Life Course*, London: Sage.

Working with babies and young children
Geraghty, P. (1988) *Caring for Children: A Textbook for Nursery Nurses*, London: Baillière Tindall.
Houghton, D. and McColgan, M. (forthcoming) *Working with Children*, London: Collins Educational.

Working with people with disabilities
Stevens, A. (ed.) (1993) *Back from the Wellhouse: Discussion Papers on Sensory Impairment and Training in Community Care Services*, London: Central Council for Education and Training in Social Work.

Working with older people
Marshall, M. (ed.) (1990) *Working with Dementia*, Birmingham: Venture Press.
Dant, T. and Gully, V. (1994) *Coordinating Care at Home*, London: Collins Educational.

6

Protecting people and preserving and promoting independence

Preview

This chapter deals with:

○ the tasks of preserving and promoting people's independence;
○ the tensions associated with protecting them.

Why is the word 'preserving' important in the title of this chapter? Why not simply refer to 'promoting' people's independence? The problem with this is that it implies that people are not independent already and do not have the autonomy to make their own choices. It is all too easy to assume, for example, that because a person is dependent in some respects on services for mobility they are in need of help to become independent. Workers should aim to empower people by working with them as persons who already possess full rights to personhood.

The protection of people is often a response to a sudden event, seen as a crisis or an emergency, such as when the worker becomes aware that people, babies and children need protection from abuse.

What does independence involve?

The move towards asserting people's autonomy, or independence, is at the heart of interaction between workers and many people. It involves two major factors:

- a tension between the *transition* from one situation to another and their empowerment in the process;
- a recognition that even people who experience a degree of dependence are already autonomous people who assert and demonstrate their full right to personhood (see Chapter 5, p. 54).

Let us examine these ideas of autonomy, transition and empowerment in more detail.

Asserting autonomy
In 1972 the first Centre for Independent Living (CIL) was established in the United States, in Berkeley, California, for disabled students and other disabled

people. By the early 1990s, there were seven CILs in Britain. Jenny Morris comments that in CILs:

> The approach is less on the actual provision of services than on ensuring that local and central government provide the housing and personal and other support services necessary for independent living. The British Council of Organizations of Disabled People has an active Independent Living Forum that forms a network of all the CILs and other organizations of disabled people that are developing independent living initiatives. This forum is also part of a European Network on Independent Living which in turn participates in the Independent Living Committee of Disabled People's International. As Rachel Hurst says, these organizations are all 'rooted in the radical move away from the traditional medical and rehabilitation professionals' control over our lives to the self-help, community-based programmes that ensure our empowerment'.

(Morris 1991, pp. 172–3)

Transition
Moving towards independence is a form of transition. Transitions, as aspects of change, inevitably involve losses and gains. Birth and death are the ultimate transitions. In largely secular Western societies, death is probably the more traumatic of these events. Work with people involves enabling them to manage their closeness to, and eventual experience of, the process of dying. Transitions, like other processes, raise emotions. Work with people involves enabling them to express and manage their emotions. It involves helping them with any difficulties they may experience associated with their emotions, and through their reactions to various circumstances in which they find themselves. The emotions linked with death include grief, anger, regret and fear, and these emotions may be expressed in different ways, such as through tears or through silence.

Empowering people
Work to enable people to become more independent is different from simply helping them. It involves resisting the impulse to make them dependent. It should empower them, rather than make them more dependent on other people than they already are. In the process, the work may enable people to:

* manage their resources;
* manage their finances;
* care for other people;
* move to a situation, physically or otherwise, where they are living more independently.

Protecting people

The most obvious and sometimes most dramatic situation demanding the immediate or future protection of people occurs when abuse becomes known to the worker. In this section, the discussion will focus on the example of the abuse of older people, for two reasons.

* Examination of child abuse often diverts attention away from other types of abuse, such as the abuse of adults.

- It helps to make the point that abuse can occur at any stage in people's lives. Bear in mind, though, that many of the points made have relevance to all work with people, whatever their age and circumstances. You should refer to the end of this chapter for further reading that compares the abuse of children and older people.

What is abuse?

There is no standard definition of abuse. Abuse of a person refers to physical, psychological, emotional, sexual or financial violation of a person's rights that causes harm, whether deliberate, unintentional, or through neglect.

What does abuse involve?

Abuse is a misuse of power. People who are abused often lack the confidence, or the will, to assert themselves and say 'no' to the abuser, or complain to somebody else. Sometimes their medical condition makes them prone to abuse, because they are unable to protest at the time or to complain afterwards. The novel *Memento Mori*, by Muriel Spark, contains some wonderfully sharp but frightening descriptions. These are of apparently insignificant actions by carers and staff, both at home and in the residential setting, which make up a variety of abusive situations. A lot of hurt can arise from a seemingly tiny act of abuse. The abuser may try to hide the abuse behind the symptoms of the person abused, or may threaten the abused person so that they are too frightened to disclose the abuse to another person. Abuse may involve a single act, or may continue over a period of time. It is not known how much abuse of older people there is. The only certainty is that a vast amount of abuse goes unreported each year.

Causes of abuse

There is no single reason why people abuse. Some abuse is by staff in a hospital, or other residential or daycare settings. Taking abuse by carers as an example, however, the most common reasons include the following:

- that the carers are under many pressures, of time and resources;
- that they are emotionally and socially isolated;
- that they do not have the emotional or practical skills to do the caring;
- that they resent being carers, but cannot avoid it;
- that they have been abused themselves;
- that their family history is disturbed in one way or another.

One type of explanation for abuse of older people suggests that it arises where the power an older person wielded over a younger relative passes over and the younger person begins to 'pay back' the older person for some previous real or imagined hurt.

Signs of abuse

Physical and emotional signs of abuse

A range of signs and symptoms may indicate that an older person is either experiencing abuse or is at risk of being abused. The following guidance published by the Social Services Inspectorate (SSI) is not comprehensive, but gives an idea of the range of things for which the worker needs to watch out when carrying out routine work.

Indicators of physical abuse

1 a history of unexplained falls or minor injuries;
2 bruising:
   (i) in well-protected areas, e.g. inside of thigh, inside of upper arm;
   (ii) bilaterally on soft parts of the body – not over bony prominences;
   (iii) clustered as from repeated striking;
3 finger marks;
4 burns in unusual location or type;
5 injuries/bruises found at different states of healing or such that it is difficult to suggest an accidental cause;
6 injury to head/face/scalp;
7 history of general practitioner or agency hopping, or episodes the accounts of which vary with the time or are inconsistent with the physical evidence, or a reluctance to seek GP services/help;
8 malnutrition when not living alone;
9 subdued personality in presence of carer;
10 ulcers, bed sores and being left in wet clothing.

Indicators of financial abuse

1 unexplained or sudden inability to pay bills;
2 unexplained or sudden withdrawal of money from accounts;
3 disparity between assets and satisfactory living conditions;
4 lack of receptivity by older person or relative to any necessary assistance requiring expenditure, when finances are not a problem (the natural thriftiness of some people should be borne in mind);
5 extraordinary interest by family members and other people in the vulnerable person's assets.

Indicators of sexual abuse

1 a change in their usual behaviour;
2 withdrawal, choosing to spend the majority of time alone;
3 overt sexual behaviour/language by the vulnerable person;
4 self-inflicted injury;
5 disturbed sleep pattern;
6 difficulty in walking, sitting;
7 torn, stained, bloody underclothes;
8 'love' bites;
9 bleeding, torn rectal and vaginal area.

Indicators of emotional abuse

1 insomnia/sleep deprivation or need for excessive sleep;
2 change in appetite;
3 unusual weight gain/loss;
4 tearfulness;
5 unexplained paranoia;
6 low self-esteem;
7 excessive fears;
8 ambivalence;
9 confusion;
10 resignation;
11 agitation.

(Tomlinson 1993, pp. 22–3)

The worker should bear in mind that the presence of at least one item on the above list should lead to the *possibility* of abuse being considered. It does not prove that abuse has occurred.

Responding to suspected abuse

Workers responding to suspected abuse must do so within the framework of relevant legislation and local procedures. Whereas the Children Act 1989 provides a comprehensive legislative framework for dealing with child abuse, the legislation drawn on in cases of the abuse of older people covers half a century. It includes the following specific measures which may be used to protect older people:

- Section 47 of the National Assistance Act 1948, which allows a person to be removed from home for up to 3 months on the grounds of protecting them;
- a modification to Section 47 of the above Act, by the National Assistance (Amendment) Act 1951, allowing a person to be removed without delay;
- guardianship under the Mental Health Act 1983;
- entry to any premises where a mentally disordered person is living, by an approved social worker, where there are grounds for believing the person is not receiving proper care;
- removing a person to a place of safety for up to 72 hours, under Section 135 of the Mental Health Act 1983;
- managing a person's financial affairs, by the Court of Protection, under Part VII of the Mental Health Act 1983 and the Court of Protection Rules 1948;
- Sections 1(2) and 9(1) of the Matrimonial Homes Act 1983, allowing the High Court and County courts to make orders enforcing or restricting the rights of spouses to occupy their matrimonial home;
- injunctions against molestation, granted by County courts under the Domestic Violence and Matrimonial Proceedings Act 1976;
- powers of magistrates' courts to make orders protecting one spouse against another, under Sections 16(2) and 16(3) of the Domestic Proceedings and Magistrates' Courts Act 1978.

The legislation also includes some general measures:

- the welfare of older people can be promoted by local authorities, under Section 45(1) of the Health Services, and Public Health Act 1968, subject to the approvals and directions of Circular LAC (93)(10);
- residential accommodation and other services can be provided under the National Assistance Act 1948, Sections 21, 26 and 29;
- local authorities are required to carry out assessments of needs where people seem to be in need of services, under the NHS and Community Care Act 1990, Section 47.

Discovery or disclosure of abuse

The knowledge that a person has abused or has been the victim of abuse may come to the worker in the normal course of events. By their nature though, many circumstances in which abuse becomes known involve some element of revelation or surprise. Sometimes the worker is told by another worker. More rarely the worker is told by a person revealing for the first time in their life the experience of having been abused. This disclosure, as it is called, will probably require the worker to follow procedures laid down by the employer locally for dealing with reported abuse. Sometimes, the situation is rather different, in that the person disclosing is an older person, and the abuse happened many decades ago, and involved one or more people now dead. This presents very different but equally complex issues and tasks that have to be tackled, perhaps as physical or emotional crises or emergencies.

Crises and emergencies

Not all crises involve emergencies. Sometimes a crisis has been in existence for some time, whereas an emergency requires immediate intervention to prevent a disaster. A crisis is a situation that will not resolve itself spontaneously. It demands some action by one or more workers and agencies, possibly involving legal intervention. Emergencies in which workers are likely to be involved range from physical situations, where first-aid skills may be needed, to those where immediate protection from an emotionally distressing situation, such as abuse, may be called for. In this second type of emergency, cooperation between different workers and agencies – such as health and social services – will be necessary in order for quick, appropriate action to be taken and further long-term work to be planned and carried out.

A calm, confident manner, even if disguising an inner nervousness, is likely to help the worker cope with an emergency. It also helps if the worker is honest and avoids deliberately giving service users and carers inaccurate or misleading information, in the misguided hope of reducing their immediate anxieties.

Enabling people to cope with transitions, losses and change

Transitions

On the positive side, transitions create opportunities, promote changes and may be welcomed by users. On the negative side, they can be very stressful, and can accelerate a person's mental and/or physical deterioration by disrupting familiar patterns of living. People experiencing transitions may welcome them, feel uncertain about them or be actively hostile towards them.

Example of a transition

People experience transition, for example, when they move from one care situation to another. In such circumstances:

- the change will need to arise from work with them;
- assessment of their situation will need to take place with them;

- the way the move is carried out will need planning with them;
- throughout the move, they will need help and support, including counselling;
- subsequently, they will need access to appropriate support and services.

Naturally, the amount and type of services needed in such a situation will vary according to individual circumstances.

Losses

Although people's impairments tend to increase with age, most older people never finish up living permanently in residential accommodation.

Impairments and disabilities of one sort or another are experienced by a significant proportion of the population. Despite this, most people do not have the opportunity to participate in making decisions about the kinds of services developed and offered to disabled people.

People with impairments or chronic illnesses, or both, often experience many losses. They have to adjust to living life as people who are marginalized, or treated as less than essential members of work, family and community groups. They may be largely or wholly excluded from personhood (see Chapter 5, p. 54, for discussion of personhood). Various treatments may involve a person experiencing difficulties through side effects. In addition, the psychological and social effects of chronic illness include living with uncertainty about one's ability to cope in the future and dealing with the responses of relatives, friends and professionals. The worker is likely to have to deal with many aspects of the impact on a family of the chronic illness of one of its members.

- Members of the family of a person who becomes chronically ill have to adjust and cope with changes to the tasks they have previously carried out.
- They probably also have to take on extra responsibilities.
- They also have to absorb the emotional impact of the illness, not only on themselves but on the person who is ill.
- The ill person may react with aggression and hostility towards other members of the household, friends, and relatives living elsewhere, perhaps as a way of coping. The reality may be that nobody is to blame for the illness, but the person's anger may need an outlet.

Working with loss: dying, death and bereavement

Change is part of life. Transitions are inevitable, as people move through life and experience changes. Death is as natural and inevitable as birth. Dying is the ultimate transition – from life to death. It involves what for most relations and friends are the most major adjustments to loss that they have to make in their lives. Some deaths of very old and terminally ill people are anticipated, and relatives and friends have the chance to prepare for the dying, the death and the period after the death. Some deaths, however, can create shock, and need to be responded to in much the same ways as other emergencies.

*A*ctivity

Consider a death, possibly of a relative, friend, service user or colleague. Try to distance yourself from the emotions you experienced at the time and respond to the following questions.

- To what extent did people who needed to grieve have time and space to do so?
- To what extent did other people make a point either of discussing the death with them or avoiding discussing it?

In Western industrialized societies, people may need help in learning how to take dying seriously. In some cultures, notably parts of white middle-class Britain, men and women who work full time may find it difficult to make the necessary space to carry out their grieving. This contrasts with Victorian society, where men and women marked the passage of time after the death of a relative by the special garments they wore, or the black fringes or patches sewn onto existing clothes. In present-day Britain such outward signs are relatively rare. Although the popularity of health and fitness diets and clubs may have much to do with personal vanity and the wish to avoid the negative impacts of physical ageing, it may also be associated with the difficulty some people experience in facing the inevitability of death. A good deal of effort goes towards extending life, and relatively little is spent dealing with dying. Those who work with people who are dying, and with their relatives and friends, will need to understand what particular physical, emotional and social demands the process of dying makes on all people involved.

Before the death

Before the death the task of the worker is to enable the dying person, and relatives and friends around them, to adjust to the situation as best suits them. They should be able to express such thoughts and feelings as they wish to.

Hospice, residential, day, home and community care for people with terminal illnesses and conditions are often concerned with the relief of pain and discomfort, rather than with prolonging effective treatments that may cause painful side effects. At the same time, there may be reasons why particular conditions need treatment during the process of dying.

Dying

Workers will need to be able to offer support and reassurance. They will also have to deal with the different circumstances and needs of the various people involved – the dying person, relatives and friends. In moving situation studies, Elisabeth Kubler-Ross shows how sensitive work can bring the dying person and their relatives and friends closer by enabling them to be open about expressing their feelings (see, for example, Kubler-Ross 1981, p. 78).

After the death

The worker will need to recognize that different people respond differently to a death. Commonly, relatives and close friends pass through a number of stages of response to death. These range from denial, through anger, to resignation and acceptance. Reactions and timescales vary enormously, however. One person may take just weeks to work through from initial anger to acceptance. Another person may still be fluctuating from one response to another many years later.

Dealing with sudden or premature deaths

Problems can arise when sudden deaths occur that do not give other people the chance to prepare themselves. Particular work may need to be done with them. An example is the family experiencing the death of a child, from an accident, from a cot death or from a long illness.

Working with people expressing emotions

Where there is silence

Silence is sometimes, but not always, a sign that people have feelings but are containing them. In work with one person, or in a group situation, silences can occur unexpectedly. The worker and other people should regard silence not necessarily as a destructive force, but as a pause, a natural break during which the person can take stock of the situation. The worker needs to recognize when silence is normal and requires no action, and when something needs doing immediately to respond to it. Of course, the worker should intervene if the other person or persons present seem to be uncomfortable and the situation needs to move on.

Where there is grief

Commonly, people express grief by crying. If one person bursts into tears, the worker should curb the following responses:

- ignoring the crying and carrying on as though it isn't happening;
- apologizing to the person crying for having brought the situation about;
- reassuring the person that everything will be fine and that there is no need to cry.

Let us take the example of one person crying. The worker's response will need to be matched to the situation, the person's needs and the reason for crying. The worker will need to recognize that sometimes crying involves the release of emotions that have built up over a long period. Three aspects are important:

1 The first thing the worker needs to do is to acknowledge, in some way, that the crying is occurring. Depending on the situation, it may or may not be appropriate for the worker to provide physical reassurance, for example, by putting an arm around the person. It all depends on the situation and on the genders and relative ages of the people concerned. A person who lives alone or is ill and who has just received very bad news is in very different circumstances to the person who is disappointed about not being able to go on an outing. The worker's response should be supportive without being oppressive.

2 The second task of the worker is to find a way to indicate to the person that they are still present and able to listen in a supportive way, if the person feels like talking. It may be sufficient for the worker to say this, and simply provide space for the person to cry.

3 Third, the worker will need to judge how quickly, and in what way, to move the situation on. Again, it depends on the circumstances. The worker may decide to leave and come back later. Or the person may benefit from talking through the tears.

The important thing is for the worker handling the situation to recognize that the professional response to crying is likely to be more controlled than the response of a relative or friend.

Where there is aggression

Aggression has many causes. These may be

- inherent in the individual;
- brought about by medication;
- part of a situation involving one or more other people;
- a feature of the culture or society in which a person has been brought up or is living.

Aggression may be expressed verbally, or through disruptive acts, including, in extreme circumstances, violence against another person. Let us consider how to respond to a person's aggression.

Responding to a display of aggression by a person

Here are some general points to bear in mind:

- avoid confronting in a threatening way, if at all possible;
- avoid standing close to, standing over, or staring at the person;
- try to respond to challenges in a calming way;
- seek help as soon as possible, from colleagues, neighbours and/or the police.

(See Department of Health Guidelines in the Further reading section at the end of this chapter.)

Responding to emotional outbursts

From time to time, most people will display emotions in outbursts, or will react strongly against somebody or something. There are two stages to the response:

1 understanding why the person reacts in this way;
2 responding.

If the worker views the person's reaction as negative, it may be more tempting for the worker to respond negatively as well. It is more helpful, however, to respond positively, or, in other words, in a *complementary* rather than a *symmetrical* way.

Symmetrical and complementary responses to aggression

Symmetrical and complementary responses to an emotional outburst by a person offer contrasting ways of dealing with them. The distinction is a particularly useful one when dealing with aggression.

A symmetrical response

A symmetrical reaction is where the worker responds by repeating the person's emotion. If the person shows anger and violence, the worker displays anger or violence in equal measure. On the whole, this response is best avoided.

A complementary response

This is more difficult. It may involve giving an indication of disapproval of the person's outburst, but leaves the way open for the worker to support the person through the emotion and find a positive outcome. In this process, the worker will need to manage the tension between setting boundaries and being sensitive to the needs of the person.

Responding to difficult situations

Consider work with a difficult situation involving a child. Three possible types of response are:

1 giving in – you can think of this as the child in you;
2 confronting, when you allow your aggression full expression.
3 standing back, yet asserting yourself; standing your ground, yet showing sensitivity to the child's feelings and wishes, without giving in.

The third response is the preferred one. Let us look at it in more detail. It involves standing back from the situation and resisting the urge to charge in. Here are some techniques associated with it:

- reframing and moving the situation on (see Chapter 1, p. 4, for discussion of this);
- using paradox, e.g. whispering not shouting;
- diversion, e.g. 'Let's do this (instead)';
- question, e.g. 'What do you want?';
- role reversal, e.g. 'What would you do if I were you?';
- withdrawal, e.g. going away and doing something else for a few minutes.

Avoid blaming and making the child feel belittled, e.g. 'You incredibly silly girl. Now look what you've done.' Blaming is likely simply to produce defensiveness, hostility and resistance to further talking on the part of the child. Try to respond in a way that:

- provides space for further interaction;
- indicates your feelings about what the child is doing;
- avoids general statements that label the child purely negatively.

Workers should always try to make statements about persons in positive rather than negative terms. Consider this example of a worker with a child.

*A*ctivity

Paulo is in a group of children. He has accidentally spilt water all over the floor, on his painting and on others on the table. He is crying, possibly in anticipation of being punished.

Negative

Now look what a mess you've made everywhere. Naughty boy!'

Positive

'Never mind. Let's mop up. The pictures will be all right.'

Now think of your own examples of negative and positive responses. It is easier to let off steam and shout at the child than to control your own emotion and think of a positive response that will anticipate other children's reactions and match the mood of the child concerned.

Methods of control

A ctivity

Consider these two examples:

1 In a group of people, of any age, there are one or two who are persistently noisy. Workers devise a response to this over time, which includes removing the person who is noisy and seating them in a special chair for five or ten minutes or so. A strap is put onto the chair to restrain the person.
2 In a nursery, for instance, a baby chair is used as a 'naughty chair', in which older children are strapped as a way of curbing their behaviour.

- Do you feel these methods of control are acceptable?
- If not, how would you respond to people who do not conform to the rules of the setting?

Physical means of control, like strapping people, whether younger or older, into a 'naughty chair', violate people's rights. They also risk escalating into even more damaging forms of control and punishment. Workers must find non-physical ways of persuading people. They should not use other physical restraints of the kind described above, except with the express approval of their line managers and employers, in line with local procedures.

Negotiating with people

A ctivity

Lena can't seem to suggest anything with which Roy, the person with whom she is working, agrees. She doesn't particularly like Roy. He is rude, he stands too close when he speaks to her, and his breath smells. She lost her temper today and nearly shouted at him.

Should she confront Roy next time he challenges her? Or should she take a 'softly, softly' approach?

(Try imagining first that Roy is another worker, then that he is a service user. How does this affect your response?)

This is a difficult dilemma. Whatever Lena does, there are risks. If she confronts Roy with her most negative, critical reactions to him, there is a danger that he will react aggressively and defensively. This may be partly as a form of denial, and partly because he may feel there is little he can do about some of her criticisms, at least in the immediate future. It is preferable for Lena to tackle with Roy the fact that they both seem to have a problem in the way they interact. Has he noticed it? If so, why does he think it happens? What can they each do about it? In the process, she may be able to address some of her other feelings with him, as they develop an increasingly open way of working together.

Preserving and promoting people's independence

It is necessary to work with all people in ways that take account of their existing level of independence. Even somebody who is quite dependent in some respects will be independent in others. Workers should resist the temptation to apply the term 'promoting independence' to all their work, since the term does not recognize the areas of people's lives in which they are independent. To summarize:

- Workers should recognize people's existing areas of independence, regardless of the level of services they need in some areas of their lives.
- Workers should provide, for people who are dependent to a greater or lesser extent, services and/or a caring and nurturing environment that promote their independence.

Over and above this, the worker needs to recognize people's differences, including cultural differences. They also need to identify and work with any special needs people may have.

The issue of people's rights is central to managing the tension between protecting them and enabling them to live more independently. The issues are fundamentally the same at any stage in life, although at different points the emphasis tends to be different. A balance has to be struck between protecting people, on the one hand, and empowering them, on the other.

Example

Mr M. uses a zimmer frame to get about. Staff invariably cannot wait for him to walk slowly from where he has been sitting to the dining area for his meal. They tend to put him into a wheelchair and push him there, to speed up the process of serving and clearing away meals.

Is it more important to clear away the breakfast things or to allow Mr M. to complete his activities in his own time?

A number of different types of impairment can affect a person's ability to live an independent life. These include physical, sensory, mental and emotional impairment.

The following areas need particular attention when working with people in situations where users are impaired:

- promoting mobility;
- maximizing flexibility and choice;
- maximizing control by users over their living space;
- enabling users to manage their own finances.

Promoting mobility

In principle, workers should aim to promote opportunities for people with impairments, which enable them to:

- maintain, and where possible improve, their mobility;
- take part in recreational and leisure activities;
- meet other people in a range of settings.

Maximizing flexibility and choice

Taking mealtimes as an example, these are some typical questions.

- Does the home or day centre enable people to choose menus and participate in preparing and serving meals?
- Do residents have a choice about when to get up, eat their meals and go to bed?

Example

Choice versus efficiency

The supply of tablecloths may be handled efficiently by the officer in charge or by ordering a batch in one design from a local supplier. It is preferable for workers to discuss with people, table by table if possible, their preferences and let each table choose a tablecloth.

Maximizing control by users over their living space

The main issues are to do with allowing people maximum control, consistent with health and safety, over the following:

- how they decorate their living space;
- how they furnish their living space;
- when their living space is cleaned – for example, they can choose not to have it cleaned when they are entertaining a friend or relative in it;
- what they choose to do in their living space.

The following situations illustrate some of these issues.

*E*xamples

Mr Q. sleeps in a room with bare painted walls, a bed, a table and a chair, already provided for him when he moved in. He was not given the choice of moving any of his own furniture or room decorations, such as pictures, with him. He was told, 'Your upholstery may create a fire hazard.' He jokingly refers to his room as 'my cell'.

Mr K. chose his curtains, rug and duvet and moved his wall clock and pictures with him when he moved in. He has his locker by his bed and his own key to a personal padlock on this.

Enabling users to manage their own finances

Priority should be given, wherever possible, to maximizing people's control over what they do with their money, including how they choose to save and spend it.

*A*ctivity

Tom is 78. His married son is unable to cope with him any longer in his house, since his own partner has become ill with a heart condition. Tom has been temporarily taken into private residential care as part of a care package. He mentions to the care worker one morning that his son is due to visit him. He wants the worker to look after his building society book for him until his son has gone. He says he fears his son will take his money and asks for advice about what to do with his investments.

   How should the worker respond?

Clearly, the worker needs to act in order to preserve Tom's rights. The worker will need also to decide how to tackle the son about the issue.

*E*xample

Here is a positive example of a person with whom staff worked carefully to maximize her independence in the transitions into and from residential care. Staff visited Mrs A. at home, to get to know her, before she arrived in a residential home, convalescing from a minor stroke. They took time and trouble to listen to her story of her life. She gave them important clues to her wishes and needs. They were able to develop a care plan with her and ensure that she lost as little independence as possible when she moved into the residential home. This made it possible for her to leave as soon as she recovered. It lessened the risk of her deteriorating and becoming a long-term resident.

The following example illustrates the tensions between health and safety and the autonomy of the service user. This issue is raised in Chapter 4.

*E*xample

Mr T. is a single man who has always cooked for himself, at home and in his work as a chef. He has been in a residential home for a month, as a short-term resident, while his carer is away on holiday. He has put in a complaint about two things:

- that he is banned from the kitchen;
- that he is not allowed to make snacks and brew up tea for himself and visitors in his own room.

The question is whether he should be given facilities to do this and whether it would make any difference if Mr T. was a long-term or permanent resident.

*A*ctivity

Mrs Fell has a learning disability. She is moving from a hostel into her own bed-sit. Draw up a checklist of things you would need to monitor, as her home care worker.

The team involved in caring for a person in, say, a residential setting may be working towards preparing them for independent living. If this is in a flat or a bed-sit, careful plans will be made. The person concerned will be involved in preparations, before and during the implementation of these plans. There will be meetings, visits to the accommodation, role plays of day-to-day living and practice in routines.

The care team should consider any changes to the care plan that this move involves. You should discuss this with them. The coordinator of the care plan or the care manager is your first point of reference.

At this point, the coordinator may decide to call a review meeting. Alternatively, the necessary consultation may take place over the phone. Somebody will need to check with the person moving what their own preferences are. It may be your task to do this.

Here are two activities based on real examples. They illustrate the tensions between running the establishment efficiently, protecting older people and taking risks that promote and assert their independence.

*A*ctivity

In a residential home for older people, the front door was locked during the day. Staff said that this was to prevent confused people wandering out and strangers wandering in. When asked what would happen if there was a fire, the officer in charge said, 'Staff all know the key is in my office, if they should need it.'

You may like to consider how you would tackle this situation.

In such a situation, it is unsafe to keep doors locked, whatever the reasons staff give for doing this. One approach is that adopted in many facilities for young children, where the door can be opened only by simultaneously turning two handles, spaced well apart. This makes it straightforward for most adults to leave the building and enables a certain amount of unrestricted access from outside. A security device on the outside of the door means that only those who know the security code can come in without having to ring the bell and wait for somebody to answer it.

Unfortunately, unless the door handles and security locks are placed conveniently, even this approach discriminates against people who cannot reach them. It could also be difficult for some people to remember the security code, and manipulate the buttons on the control panel, when they wanted to open the door.

*A*ctivity

A social services department announced in the early 1990s that it would tag elderly people in its residential establishments. This was to prevent somebody dying out of the reach of staff help. Tagging involves attaching a small transmitter to a person, so that their movements can be followed from a monitoring point.

What are the arguments for and against this proposal?

Perhaps you can suggest alternative ways of responding to the problem.

When the tagging suggestion was tried in the field of criminal justice, as an alternative to locking up some offenders, many practical problems, not to say the expense of the scheme, made it unattractive to many people. Practical problems apart, it contradicts the principles of people's rights and non-discriminatory practice set out in Chapter 1, p. 0.

An alternative response to this problem is for the authorities to provide people with fixed and mobile telephones and alarms, which they can activate simply. These can be used if they get into difficulties and want to summon help. This uses technology appropriately. It may actually give some residents confidence to live more independently on a day-to-day basis, because they know they can call for help if they need it.

Key questions

Use these questions to check back over the material covered in the chapter and assess your grasp of it, before moving on. Discuss the questions, and responses to them, with colleagues and tutors.

○ What is the range of signs and symptoms of physical abuse of a person?
○ What are the main stages through which a person passes in response to bereavement?
○ What responses to a person's aggression are preferable to a symmetrical reaction?
○ Can you give examples of when liberation and protection of children may be appropriate?
○ What are the main skills associated with living independently?

Relevant GNVQ/SNVQ and NVQ/SVQ Units

The material in this chapter will help with preparation for the following Health and Social Care GNVQ/SNVQ Units

Intermediate Level:

Unit 3 – Health and emergencies
Advanced Level:
Unit 2 – Interpersonal interaction
and NVQ/SVQ Units from the following National Occupational Standards
for Care:
    Key role W – Support the maintenance and development of client identity and relationships
    Key role Y – Support clients in developing self-sufficiency
for Working with Young Children:
    C.10 – Promote children's sensory and intellectual development
    C.11 – Promote the development of children's language and communication skills
    C.14 – Care for and promote the development of babies
    C.15 – Contribute to the protection of children from abuse

Further reading

Doyle, C. (1990) *Working with Abused Children*, London: Macmillan. (An excellent source of practical help.)

Jones, D.N. *et al.* (eds) (1987) *Understanding Child Abuse*, London: Macmillan. (A comprehensive source of material on theories and practice.)

Department of Health (1991) *Working Together: A Guide to Arrangements for Inter-agency Co-operation for the Protection of Children from Abuse* (2nd edn), London: HMSO. (A comprehensive source book for information about child abuse work.)

Department of Health (1992) *Child Protection: Guidance for Senior Nurses, Health Visitors and Midwives*, London: HMSO. (Specific guidance for health service professionals.)

Department of Health and Social Security Guidelines (Ref. HC76/11). (This contains advice on how to deal with people acting aggressively and violently.)

Working with people before, during and after a death
Kubler-Ross, E. (1981) *Living with Death and Dying*, London: Souvenir Press.

Stoddard, S. (1978) *The Hospice Movement: A Better Way of Caring for the Dying*, London: Jonathan Cape. (A good introduction to the work of hospices.)

Age Concern, Scotland (1987) *Residential Care: Is It For Me?*, Edinburgh: HMSO. (A good guide to decisions, issues and tasks facing service users and carers considering residential care.)

Ramon, S. (ed.) (1991) *Beyond Community Care: Normalization and Integration Work*, London: MIND/Macmillan.

Stevens, A. (ed.) (1993) *Back from the Wellhouse: Discussion Papers on Sensory Impairment and Training in Community Care Services*, London: Central Council for Education and Training in Social Work. (A good source of material on work with Deaf, blind and partially sighted people and people with multiple impairments.)

Tomlinson, D.F. (1993) *No Longer Afraid: The Safeguard of Older People in Domestic Settings*, London: HMSO. (This is guidance published by the Social Services Inspectorate on how to deal with the abuse of older people. It contains very useful material comparing abuse of children with abuse of older people.)

First aid

Look in the phone books for the nearest branch of the British Red Cross Society, St John's Ambulance, St Andrew's Ambulance Association, or write to the Royal Society for the Prevention of Accidents (RoSPA), Cannon House, The Priory, Queensway, Birmingham, B4 6BS.

Caring For the Sick, Nursing the Ill, the Disabled, Children and the Elderly (1988) (2nd edn), The Authorized Manual of St John Ambulance, St Andrew's Ambulance, The British Red Cross Society.

Emergency Procedures for Everyone at Home, at Work or at Leisure (1987), The Authorized Manual of St. John Ambulance, St. Andrew's Ambulance Association, the British Red Cross Society.

7

Becoming competent in work with people

Preview

This chapter:

○ provides basic information about what competence is and the components of competence;

○ explores National Vocational Qualifications / Scottish Vocational Qualifications (NVQ/SVQ) as an approach to competence in working with people;

○ discusses the opportunities for, barriers to, and ways of learning about working with people;

○ deals with decisions and issues encountered in using NVQs/SVQs as a means of qualifying as a competent worker.

What is competence?

Becoming competent involves demonstrating the ability to use knowledge (including legal knowledge), values and skills in the work. Some workers acquire competence simply through doing their job. Others gain a qualification at the same time as being involved in this process. Those learning at work tend to be adult learners who have been away from formal education since their school days.

More likely than not, the task of becoming qualified through NVQs/SVQs in work with people will be carried out when an individual is already doing the work. Most students of work with people will want to improve their effectiveness in what they are already doing.

Why is competence important?

Since the early 1980s, there has been a trend in many trades towards specifying what makes for good practice. Since working with people is in many ways more complex than working with things, it is easier to achieve this in, for example, plumbing than in working with people. However, the prevailing view is that workers in any field need to know what good practice entails. This is so that consistently high standards can be set and monitored according to agreed criteria. After all, a scandal due, say, to the failure of care workers to carry out their responsibilities is just as damaging, and many people would argue more so, than burst water pipes due to a plumber not lagging them in a frosty area. Water can be mopped up. The scars from emotional and physical harm to a person can take generations to heal.

The pressure to specify competent practice has thus come about partly through the general trend in different trades and professions towards establishing standards. It has also come about through the reactions of people, professionals, commentators and the mass media to various scandals and inquiries into a wide range of services.

For instance, complaints about the treatment of patients in Rampton special hospital led to an inquiry report and staff being convicted (DHSS 1980). There was also pressure to improve training of workers in the fields of learning disability and mental health.

Another example is the abduction on 14 August 1992 of a baby by a person claiming to be a child-minder. This led to increased pressure towards compulsory registration of all carers for children. At that time, the registration of all child-minders by local authorities, required by the Children Act 1989, was still not complete, and nannies and baby-sitters were still not required to be registered. Registration of workers usually accompanies improved standards of education, training and practice. In 1992, it became clear that child-minders would have to meet NVQ/SVQ standards and that special standards referring to this work would need to be developed.

*A*ctivity

Think of some events that cause standards of work with people to be scrutinized.

Here are some examples:

- suicides in prisons (see, for instance, Scottish Home and Health Department 1985), which raise questions about how staff deal with people who threaten suicide;
- bullying at school, associated with poor teaching, according to Her Majesty's Inspectors (*Guardian*, 8 December 1993);
- the death of a child through abuse (see, for instance, report of public inquiry into death of Tyra Henry: Arnold *et al.* 1987);
- the sudden deaths of hospital patients/residents in homes for older people;
- a series of salmonella and food poisoning outbreaks in establishments for people.

Debates about the NVQ/SVQ approach tend to focus on its alleged strengths and weaknesses. Here are some of the main arguments.

Supporters of the NVQ/SVQ approach advocate:

- the attraction of a single standard for describing jobs, training and services for people;
- a value base threaded through functional areas of performance;

- an emphasis on performance and 'knowledge for' the job;
- work performance defined according to levels based on the nature of the job;
- greater clarity about standards of work and clarity about what is to be done by staff;
- an emphasis on the supervision of staff, linked with the learning process;
- a range of specified methods of gathering evidence;
- a single standard of performance across a range of care situations.

Critics of the NVQ/SVQ approach refer to:

- the risk of particular skills becoming dominant and a neglect of understanding and critical reflection;
- problems of the overuse of technical jargon in the standards produced by NCVQ;
- the risk of an emphasis on competence being parcelled up into chunks of values, knowledge and skills;
- the difficulty of specifying when tasks are complex, e.g. at the higher NVQ/SVQ Levels;
- problems of lack of resources to supervise and assess the performance of people in the workplace;
- risks of accepting the status quo in the workplace instead of looking ahead and striving for the best possible practice.

There are two further complications.

1 NVQs/SVQs are not universally accepted or adopted by all service providers. There is a gradual spread of NVQs/SVQs, but there is a low take-up of the approach in some sectors and organizations, which partly reflects technical problems of setting up assessment arrangements and so forth. There are also problems with resourcing training for staff as well as resistance to the NVQ/SVQ approach itself from some individuals and organizations.
2 The character of work varies in different sectors. This affects the qualifications offered for different competences. For example, the health services in Britain are more unified than the personal social services, in terms of the ways services are organized and provided and in the range of accredited qualifications. In the social care field, there are several accrediting bodies for qualifications.

Whatever the merits of these arguments, there is no doubt of the general benefits to workers of the competence-based approach of the NCVQ. Through it, workers are likely to receive training, support and supervision while on the job. They will also be assessed to a generally agreed standard of competence in carrying out their daily work.

*A*ctivity

Try listing ways in which a published checklist of the values, knowledge and skills making for competent care work could help the following:

- a service user;
- a worker;
- a manager;
- an organization.

You may find it helpful to discuss your responses with colleagues and/or fellow students.

Many courses – one standard of qualification

The main bodies that provide courses differ, but the NVQs to which these courses relate provide an unchanging standard against which to judge the competence of a candidate for assessment. For example, Business Technician Education Council (BTEC), English Nursing Board (ENB), Central Council for Education and Training in Social Work (CCETSW) and City and Guilds of London Institute all provide qualifications related to NVQs in integrated caring.

What makes for competent work with people?

We shall now examine in more detail these three inseparable elements of competent work.

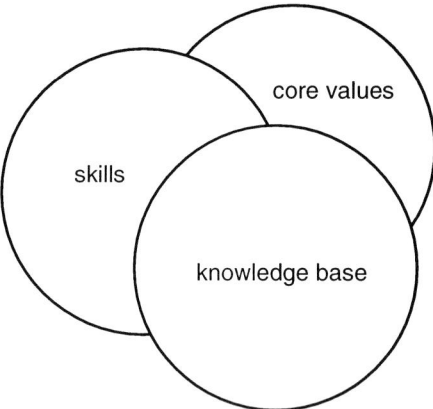

In order to demonstrate competence, values, knowledge and skills must be integrated. Integration refers to the process of mixing the three elements together so thoroughly that in practice, each element draws on and contributes to the other two elements. Let's examine the three elements in turn.

Values

A value is a highly regarded, essential feature of all practice.

Similar NVQ/SVQ statements of core values and principles underpin and permeate all the different qualifications and endorsements. This has been dealt with in Chapter 1 (pp. 5–6).

Knowledge

Surely, we all know what knowledge is? Why spend time writing about it? The reason is that the word 'knowledge' covers a range of things, from being able to recite something 'parrot-fashion' to having a critical understanding of it and being able to use that understanding in the work situation.

Working with people requires knowledge in the latter sense. For example, we draw on knowledge of the law, the organizational setting in which we do the work, the society in which we live, the culture of our workplace and the people with whom we work. The word 'culture' refers here to the beliefs and practices of the workplace.

Skills

It is easier to give an example of a skill than it is to specify what constitutes skilled work.

Examples of skills include making relationships, assessing needs, listening and making good decisions. In each of these areas, the element of interaction with other people is impossible to quantify and requires a judgement about its quality.

A ctivity

Use the following headings to carry out a quick analysis of the components of competence of your own job:

- values;
- knowledge;
- skills.

Let's bring together the analysis of the components of competence outlined above with the description here and in Chapter 1 (pp. 3–9) of the essentials of reflective anti-oppressive practice.

Becoming reflective involves you in:

- self-development of you as a whole person;
- thinking about what you are doing;
- analysing and understanding what you are doing;
- developing self-awareness;
- improving your sensitivity to other people;
- using your reflections to help your future practice.

Becoming competent involves you as a reflective worker:

- in developing and using your value base, by:
  - recognizing the components of your value base;
  - identifying areas of uncertainty, ethical dilemmas, conflict and change;
  - using your values as the basis of your work;
  - adopting values in practice (see Chapter 1, pp. 4–5) that guide all your work;
- in developing and using your knowledge base, by:
  - appraising strengths and gaps in your knowledge;
  - identifying relevant knowledge for you to acquire;

- reading, watching and listening critically;
- finding out where to find relevant knowledge, without having to memorize it all;
- using what you know to help your work;
- in developing and using your skills in:
  - sensitivity and self-awareness;
  - assertiveness, decisiveness and reliability;
  - interpersonal work with individual people;
  - working with people in groups;
  - openness;
  - planning;
  - assessing;
  - carrying out;
  - bringing to a conclusion;
  - evaluating how you feel, think and act (this is often called self-evaluation);
  - evaluating the outcomes of what you do.

This is a very daunting list. The variety of work settings and jobs produces a great variety of challenges in different areas of expertise.

*A*ctivity

Examine an organization with which you are familiar. List examples of key staff at senior, middle and junior levels. Estimate how much time per day they spend talking with service users at each level.

Consider, for example, a hospital ward. Which staff have most day-to-day involvement with patients: consultants or health care assistants?

Often, the more junior staff in subordinate positions in the organization are the ones who have the greatest exposure to users of the services. Forming and sustaining effective working relationships with people is central to the work. On the other hand, more senior staff will be concerned with more complex tasks involving managing and coordinating.

Let us now examine how the competences for working with people have been developed and structured.

What are National Vocational Qualifications / Scottish Vocational Qualifications (NVQs/SVQs)?

In July 1986, the Government announced in the White Paper, *Working Together – Education and Training*, its intention to set up the National Council for Vocational Qualifications (NCVQ). Its task was to develop a framework for National Vocational Qualifications (NVQs) covering England, Wales and Northern Ireland. In Scotland, as part of the Scottish Action Plan, the Scottish Vocational Educational Council (SCOTVEC) developed Scottish Vocational

Qualifications (SVQs). These are assured by SCOTVEC and NCVQ to be equivalent to NVQs.

Each sector of employment has a lead body. The industry lead body for care is the Care Sector Consortium / Occupational Standards Council (CSC/OSC).

Responsibility for devising and assessing standards of competence is being allocated to various bodies, as these standards are developed. In England and Wales responsibility has been given to the Local Government Management Board (LGMB) and the National Health Service Training Authority (NHSTA). Although SVQs and NVQs are developed for Scotland and for England and Wales respectively, they are still each valid as qualifications recognized throughout the UK.

The development of work-based assessment of workers' competence based on NVQs/SVQs has changed the relationship between colleges and employers. NVQs/SVQs represent a trend towards qualifications that employers anticipate will meet workforce needs.

Here are some examples of NVQs/SVQs

Care awards
Health care assistants and care assistants can hold NVQ qualifications in care at Level 2. They are trained mainly on the job – in the ward, establishment or office where they work – with some off-the-job training while released from work.

Child care and education awards
These are for those who work with children under 7 and their families in settings such as nurseries and playgroups.

Criminal justice service awards
Standards in criminal justice services have been developed at Levels 3 and 4, for workers in community and residential settings, such as hostels.

Occupational standards

NVQs/SVQs are being set out in most trades and professions. Those in 'working with people' are produced under different categories, depending on what sort of work is done and the level of competence required.

Each NVQ/SVQ consists of a list of competences the worker must demonstrate in order to obtain it. The different qualifications can be gained at different Levels.

The contents of the National Occupational Standards published so far in the area of work with people are as follows:

National Occupational Standards for Working with Young Children and their Families

C.2   Care for children's physical needs
C.3   Promote the physical development of young children

C.4, C.5   Support children's social and emotional development
C.6   Contribute to the management of children's behaviour
C.7   Provide for the management of children's behaviour
C.8   Set out and clear away play activities
C.9   Work with young children
C.10   Promote children's sensory and intellectual development
C.11   Promote the development of children's language and communication skills
C.12   Feed babies
C.13   Care for babies
C.14   Care for and promote the development of babies
C.15   Contribute to the protection of children from abuse
C.16   Observe and assess the development and behaviour of children
E.1   Maintain a child-orientated environment
E.2   Maintain the safety of children
M.1   Give administrative and technical support on request
M.2   Carry out the administration of the provision for a care/education setting
M.3   Work under the direction of others
M.4   Work with colleagues in a team
M.7   Plan, implement and evaluate activities and experiences to promote children's learning and development
M.8   Plan, implement and evaluate routines of young children
M.20   Work with/to a management committee

National Occupational Standards for Care

Value base unit O   Promote equality for all individuals
Key role U   Contribute to the maintenance of an environment for effective care
Key role V   Contribute to the planning, delivery and evaluation of services which provide support and care
Key role W   Support the maintenance and development of client identity and relationships
Key role X   Support clients during specific treatment, therapeutic and development programmes
Key role Y   Support clients in developing self-sufficiency
Key role Z   Support and promote clients' independence in situations of dependency

Awards in criminal justice service

Level 3: Core Units

O   Promote equality for all individuals
U.4   Contribute to the health, safety and security of individuals and their environment
U.5   Obtain, transmit and store information relating to the delivery of a care service

V.1   Contribute to the planning and monitoring of service delivery
Y.2   Enable clients to make use of available services and information
Z.1   Contribute to the protection of individuals from abuse
Z.3   Contribute to the management of aggressive and abusive behaviour
C.J1   Support individuals experiencing difficulties
C.J2   Contribute in assisting individuals to address offending behaviour
C.J3   Contribute to effective team practice

Option sets

Individual support and development (any 4 of the 6 Units)
W.5   Support clients with difficulties or potentially difficult relationships
X.2   Prepare and provide agreed individual development activities for clients
Y.3   Enable clients to administer their financial affairs
Z.2   Contribute to the provision of advocacy for clients
Z.18   Support clients who are substance users
Z.18   Support individuals where abuse has been disclosed

Agency services (any 4 of the 6 Units)
C.J4   Represent agency at a formal hearing
C.J5   Contribute to the development of agency policy and practice
C.J7   Arrange individuals' entry to, and moving on from, agency services
C.J7   Contribute to the supervision of court orders and post-custody statutory requirements
C.J8   Maintain work placements
C.J9   Provide work placement supervision

Level 4

O   Promote equality for all individuals
U.4   Contribute to the health, safety and security of individuals and their environment
U.5   Obtain, transmit and store information relating to the delivery of a care service
M.13   Recommend, monitor and control the use of resources
M.15   Develop teams, individuals and self to enhance performance
M.16   Plan, allocate and evaluate work carried out by teams, individuals and self
C.J5   Contribute to the development of agency policy and practice
C.J10 Assist individuals in their personal development and relationships with others
C.J11 Assist individuals to understand and address their difficulties
C.J12 Assist individuals to address offending behaviour
C.J13 Assess individuals needs and plan service delivery
C.J14 Assist individuals with negotiations and formal hearings
C.J15 Manage abusive and aggressive behaviour
C.J16 Assist in the management of conflict
C.J19 Market agency services
C.J20 Develop inter-agency and community responses to crime

Additional Units
C.J17 Supervise court orders
C.J18 Assist individuals to make reparation for offending behaviour
C.J21 Manage and maintain project accommodation services
C.J22 Establish and implement contractual arrangements for the use and occupation of accommodation

Levels of NVQ/SVQ

There are five different Levels of NVQ/SVQ. The NVQs/SVQs offer a structure of qualifications, from general supporting roles at Level 1 through to a professional qualification at Level 5. The Level 3 award is at the minimum entry requirements for starting a qualifying course or programme in such professions as chiropody, physiotherapy or social work. NVQ Levels as set out by the NCVQ are as follows.

Level 1: competence in the performance of a range of varied work activities, most of which may be routine and predictable.

Level 2: competence in a significant range of varied work activities, performed in a variety of contexts. Some of the activities are complex or non-routine, and there is some individual responsibility or autonomy. Collaboration with others, perhaps through membership of a work group or team, may often be a requirement.

Level 3: competence in a broad range of varied work activities performed in a variety of contexts and most of which are complex and non-routine. There is considerable responsibility and autonomy, and control or guidance of others is often required.

Level 4: competence in a broad range of complex, technical or professional work activities performed in a wide variety of contexts and with a substantial degree of personal responsibility and autonomy. Responsibility for the work of others and the allocation of resources is often present.

Level 5: competence that involves the application of a significant range of fundamental principles and complex techniques across a wide and often unpredictable variety of contexts. Very substantial personal autonomy and often significant responsibility for the work of others and for the allocation of substantial resources feature strongly, as do personal accountabilities for analysis and diagnosis, design, planning, execution and evaluation.

(*NVQ Monitor*, September 1992, p. 12)

General National Vocational Qualifications (GNVQs) provide a vocational alternative to GCSEs and A-levels. One of the subject areas is Health and Social Care. GNVQs are available at three levels, including Intermediate (GCSE equivalent) and Advanced (A-level equivalent). GNVQ students are assessed on a portfolio of project work in school or college and an externally devised set test. GNVQs/GSVQs:

- are vocationally based;
- include core skills in communication, application of number, information technology, personal and interpersonal skills, problem solving;
- allow people to progress to higher level qualifications.

Two units called Skills Start 1 and 2 also precede entry to either SVQ or National Certificate. These are for people with learning difficulties and for people who have been out of work for some time or who lack confidence.

The statements of competence that make up NVQs/SVQs have been based on the key aspects of specific jobs. These are constructed in a particular way. A worker's competence is assessed against clusters of competences called units. Each competence is reached by analysing jobs in caring and grouping them together in key roles. The assessment of workers' competence is based on how they perform, measured against standard performance criteria. NVQ candidates have to demonstrate that they have attained every element of competence – that is, met every one of the performance criteria – in order to gain an award at that Level.

Performance criteria

NVQs/SVQs are based on several layers, rather like building blocks:

NVQ/SVQ
Unit of competence
Element of competence
Performance criterion

A performance criterion is a standard by which a candidate's performance at work is judged.

An element of competence is a collection of performance criteria.

A unit of competence comprises a number of elements of competence.

An NVQ/SVQ is assessed in terms of a number of units of competence.

Learning barriers, opportunities and methods

Barriers to learning

Those wanting to improve their competence in working with people are likely to encounter a number of difficulties.

The barriers to learning reflect divisions in society as a whole, in organizations and institutions, in groups and between individual people. They are not always obvious but their effects may be powerful and negative. There are, of course, divisions and inequalities in the workforces caring for people throughout their life courses. These divisions and inequalities are reflected in the struggles many people have to become qualified and demonstrate their competence. Barriers partly reflect how people feel, as well as their objective circumstances.

Consider the examples below. You could discuss with colleagues the various difficulties each person may face.

In each case, complete the sentence, 'The barriers to learning I face are . . . '

*E*xamples

I am a 40-year-old woman who left school with no formal qualifications. I have been working on shifts as an auxiliary in a hospital. People say to me, 'surely you aren't going back to college.'

I am an 18-year-old black African Caribbean male. I have tried several times to get into the police and prison service, but have been turned down. I work as a health care assistant.

My husband and children are very demanding. My husband says he wants me to work, but whenever I open a worksheet or anything I've brought home from work, I am made to feel guilty that I'm not on my feet doing housework.

I regard myself as a disabled person. I work in a day centre for older people. I find getting to and from book shops and libraries very difficult, and I want to get trained.

With the children and my mother in the house all the time, it's impossible even to think about work when I'm at home, let alone read or write anything.

Use the following activity to reflect on your own situation.

*A*ctivity

Write a sentence or two describing the main barriers to learning that you have, or have had to overcome.

Here is a list of possible factors that may create problems for learners:

- the difficulties of part-time study;
- a lack of somewhere to study, at work/at home;
- the fact that learning disturbs established household activities and relationships;
- a lack of confidence about coping;

- isolation from other like-minded people;
- extra travelling to college;
- overwork;
- a lack of support at home;
- a lack of sympathy and sharing chores at home;
- anxieties about being shown up and/or failing in a group of fellow learners.

Peter Marris argues that many women who are motivated towards pursuing personal and professional development through vocational courses have to face particular problems and contradictions. These include the lack of equivalent rewards comparable with their male counterparts and also the clash with the conventional expectations of their feminine roles (Marris 1992, p. 143). An ambitious woman is more likely to be criticized for neglecting her family and children than an ambitious man.

The Social Services Inspectorate (SSI) has produced a very critical report. It highlights the need for managers and workers to be committed to the belief that 'women's contributions are of equal value at all levels in the organization and that caring responsibilities should not be a deterrent to full participation in the workforce' (SSI 1991a, p. 56).

Learning opportunities

Learning opportunities may be there, in the work setting, or they may need developing or creating. Aspects of learning opportunities may need to be worked at. It may be a struggle to create some of them.

The fact that each worker has a unique background of previous learning and experience makes it likely that the opportunities for learning how to work with people will vary widely. They will depend on the baseline of needs established by the worker's learning profile (see below for discussion of this) and any barriers to learning that may exist.

The worst possibility is that learning opportunities will not exist. There may be no paid work, no voluntary work and the nearest college or library may be too far away, or physically inaccessible for reasons other than distance alone.

Learning opportunities may need to be developed. This may involve creating or improving them, to avoid anyone being in the 'worst possible' situation described above. The development of learning opportunities will be necessary also to ensure, for example, that the principles of working with people are learned.

Constructing a learning profile

It will be helpful to start by establishing a baseline of learning needs. This is done by reviewing previous learning and experience and constructing a portfolio illustrating its relevance to the standards against which the worker is claiming competence.

Previous learning and experience
Learning is a mixture of formal and informal experiences. What one person views as useful experience another may regard as a waste of time. Formal

learning includes schooling, and further and higher education. Schooling may be primary, secondary and tertiary. Formal learning about work with people, involving work and education, may be linked with a relevant course of study, such as:

- BTEC First Certificate in Caring;
- BTEC National Certificate in Nursery Nursing;
- BTEC National Certificate in Social Care;
- BTEC First Diploma Caring;
- BTEC National Diploma Caring Services (Social Care);
- BTEC National Diploma Caring Science (Health Studies);
- BTEC National Diploma Caring Services (Nursery Nursing);
- BTEC Higher National Diploma in Caring Services;
- CGLI 324–1 Certificate in Caring for Children;
- CGLI 325–1 Certificate in Community Care Practice;
- CGLI 325–2 Certificate in Foundation Management for Care;
- CGLI 325–3 Certificate in Advanced Care Management;
- Diploma in Post Qualifying Studies (NNEB);
- CGLI 331 Family and Community Care;
- Pre-Nursing Course;
- National Nursery Examination Board Diploma/Pre-Diploma;
- Intermediate GNVQ Health and Social Care;
- Advanced GNVQ Health and Social Care;
- BTEC Higher National Diploma in Caring Services (Social Care, Health Care and Child Care);
- PPA Diploma Course;
- National Nursery Examination Board Diploma/Pre-Diploma;
- Diploma in Care Management;
- Certificate in Health Services Management / Health and Social Services Management;
- Diploma in Health Services Management / Health and Social Services Management;
- MESOL/Advanced MESOL.

APEL and CATS

The accreditation of prior learning (APEL) involves putting together a statement, usually in the form of a portfolio. It normally contains evidence of previous learning and experience, relevant to the task now being assessed. It should go part of the way towards meeting some of the assessment requirements.

Some learners undertake formally assessed programmes or courses. These may be linked with arrangements for credit to be acquired, accumulated and transferred as a learner moves from one learning setting to another. This process is known as a credit accumulation and transfer scheme (CATS).

Claiming competence through a portfolio

A portfolio may be compiled by a worker to contribute to the process of assessing prior learning (APL). Once APL has been carried out, the gaps in relevant experience and learning are clear and a learning contract can be drawn up. A portfolio is a systematic collection of the evidence of a worker's achievements. A candidate for assessment must provide current evidence of performance, in addition to the portfolio, in order to gain certification for any unit of competence.

A typical portfolio is likely to contain:

- background information about the award sought, the assessment centre, the assessor, and the units sought;
- relevant information about the candidate's experience, separately listing each area of achievement and its supporting evidence;
- evidence, including:
  - certificates from courses attended, if work-based tasks have been accomplished within them;
  - outcomes of experience;
  - written references, endorsements and recommendations, for example from employers;
- a record of new information emerging during the interview with the assessor;
- a record of progress made since the interview with the assessor.

The words 'relevant previous experience' refer to the fact that everyone has experiences in life. The issue is what we gain from them and how we use what we have gained. Some older people have decades of experience but have not learned from them. Some very young people seem able to gain benefit from short experiences. Some short experience is varied and relevant; other experience is lengthy, but irrelevant.

We shall now look at the curriculum vitae as a systematic way of organizing the recording of relevant information.

The curriculum vitae

Some people use the term curriculum vitae (CV) to describe the summary statement of a person's learning and experience to date.

Here is a checklist of items that normally would be part of a CV:

- full name;
- address at work and at home with telephone numbers where appropriate;
- date of birth, bearing in mind that some people object to including this in a CV as a matter of course, on equal opportunities grounds;
- schooling, including the dates of periods spent in secondary schools, the name(s) of the school(s) and subjects titles, dates, and levels of any qualifications obtained;
- further/higher education, including details of colleges, courses taken, certificates and/or qualifications;
- paid employment, starting with the present job and working backwards, giving details of each employer's name and address, the dates and any details briefly clarifying what the job involved;
- hobbies and interests;
- references, including those for the most recent experiences, whether as employee, volunteer or student.

*A*ctivity

Draft your own CV, using the following headings: Name, Address, Date of birth, Education, Employment, Interests and References.
   Incorporate your CV into a portfolio. Discuss your plans and drafts with a colleague.

Learning needs and learning objectives

The learning profile is a statement of the areas of learning that require greater or less attention. It is used to make decisions about what values, knowledge and skills need improving in order to prioritize the learning aims on which you concentrate. Everyone's learning profile is unique to them and will change through time.

The next task is to seek opportunities for learning. More often than not, some barriers to learning will need to be overcome before the learning opportunities can be developed and used.

There is no single, 'right' way to learn

People learn in different ways and at different speeds. Adults have the opportunity to select for themselves what they choose to learn and how they learn it. Many adults who have been away from formal teaching and learning in the classroom for many years are likely to have had a fairly mixed or even negative experience of schooling. Often, a worker will be able to use workplace experiences to learn about work-based issues and to develop practice competence.

Adult learning in the workplace is likely to be most effective when the worker:

- feels able to take responsibility for what is learned;
- feels motivated by a task or a problem that needs tackling;
- wants to improve self-confidence, assertiveness, self-esteem and fulfilment;
- has adequate support at work, from a mentor or supervisor;
- has a line manager who is supportive;
- meets and discusses learning issues and problems with other workers.

How to study

Different people learn and study differently, and the same person can learn differently in different circumstances. Here are some general guidelines on how to study.

Make space to study

- Set aside study time.
- Be practical.
- Cut out distractions, such as people, the telephone, windows, pets, hunger, cold, the TV and radio.
- Plan.
- Get access to necessary materials, such as books and articles.

Choose to study when your mind is at its most alert

- Divide your study time into short, intensive, productive sessions.
- Be as active as possible in the way you learn. You will learn best by doing.
- Assess what you need to know.
- Don't work for too long.
- Set goals that are achievable at a single sitting.
- Concentrate for a short period, then take a break.
- Explore issues arising from your learning in discussion with other people.
- Talk.
- Listen.
- Keep notes.

Learn knowledge for the purpose of improving your competence

- Allow time to think.
- Get support.
- Keep in touch with other learners.
- Share experiences and support with each other when the studying is hard.
- Manage the tension between maintaining a sharp focus on the subject and thinking and reading in an open-ended way to help the flow of ideas.
- Develop the habit of reading a broadsheet daily and/or Sunday newspaper (*The Times, The Independent, Telegraph, Guardian, Sunday Observer, Sunday Times, Sunday Telegraph*).
- Keep press cuttings that interest you; date them and stick them in a scrapbook.
- Develop the habit of regularly browsing through professional journals that are relevant to your area, and reading particular articles that apply to your work.

Identify, and maximize the benefit from the different skills involved in studying:

Activity	Skills involved
Reading	
Writing	taking notes; writing up assignments; writing reports
Discussion	asking; answering; listening; asserting; accepting criticism
Describing	observing events
Interpreting	judging
Evaluating	concept-utilizing; theorizing; evaluating policies and practice
Self-evaluating	evaluating own ideas, own feelings and own work

Reading a book, article, or other document

Here is the sequence of activity involved in reading some material.

- Survey what the piece of reading is about.
- Read small chunks.
- Note key points.
- Pose questions to yourself.
- Answer them as well as possible.
- Recall key points: ask yourself what you can remember?
- Read the next chunk: go back over the text and note any points missed or wrongly recalled.

Developing competence is a lifelong learning process

The development of competence is a lifelong process. It involves becoming reflective about the values, knowledge and skills expressed in practice. Practice isn't just about tasks carried out. It involves you and me as thinking and feeling people (see Chapter 1, pp. 3–4). Developing reflective practice will have an impact on you and on me, not just now but, once we adopt the approach, for the rest of our lives.

The worker who is becoming competent will be able to recognize that this is happening because, inevitably, reflection has an impact on the worker as a whole person, and not just during the hours of work. This is not to advocate that you as the worker take work home with you. However, putting into practice the principles of working with people is bound to affect the worker as a person. Typical signs are aspects learned at work that get carried over into personal life. This is more likely to be a feature of learning how to work with people than in, for example, a trade like plumbing, since sensitivity and self-awareness have to be part of the stock in trade of those who work with people. It is also more likely because issues affecting work with people are all around us, as part of everyday life – when we see a person with an impairment waiting at the kerb as we cross the street, when we see a neighbour smacking a child severely, when a friend or relative has a stroke, or when an item about child abuse makes news headlines. Let us consider now how a worker may demonstrate competence in an NVQ.

How to achieve an NVQ/SVQ

Candidates for awards do not all have to work up from Level 1. They can enter at the Level that most suits their needs. The worker is likely to benefit from entry at the Level at which they are already working and/or are judged competent.

A candidate for an SVQ, for example, registers with SCOTVEC, pays a registration fee and buys a record book. This book is used as the basis for charting the candidate's progress, in relation to national standards of competence. People may either demonstrate competence and gain credit for one or two units, or work towards a full qualification.

A worker needs to demonstrate the following in order to claim an NVQ/SVQ:

- that they understand what the award is;
- that they understand how the units and elements of the award are structured;
- that they know how to collect evidence of their competence for each unit;
- that they know how the units combine to form an award.

Are any elements of competence optional?
None of the elements of competence laid down for NVQs/SVQs is negotiable. That is, all of them have to be demonstrated in order for the candidate to be awarded an NVQ/SVQ.

Making the most of work-based learning

There are two kinds of work-based learning:

- learning for general work experience;
- learning for NVQ/SVQ candidates.

Work experience placements

A ctivity

Starting a placement

Zoë was attached to a day nursery for infants and children, for work experience. What would be the best way for her to introduce herself to the work:

1 to spend all the time playing with the children and ignoring the other workers;
2 to spend all the time chatting to the other workers and ignoring the children;
3 to decide in advance to divide the time equally between talking to the other workers and playing with children;
4 to start by playing with the children, then alternate between chatting to staff and playing with the children;
5 to start by talking to other workers and agreeing how to introduce herself through playing with the children?

It is important to plan, review and evaluate work experience and agree at the start how this will be done. The worker should adopt a working style that is appropriate for the setting and that suits them. Planning, reviewing and evaluating should be carried out against criteria for performance. An attempt should be made to work (and this includes play!) purposefully. The key is to avoid being a wallflower.

Workers will find keeping a diary useful. Some people call this a self-development log. In the diary, try to make five kinds of notes:

1 notes about things that happen;
2 records of any discoveries you have made;
3 your reflections on those things;

4 relevant information and any specific knowledge you come across in the day;
5 your comment later about what kind of day it was.

Friday April 30

Events

Discoveries

Thoughts

Information

Later comments

The worker will find it useful to refer back to the log at a later date. It will help in thinking about what is being done. It will also provide a source of information about the work done.

The following questions will help you to reflect on the work done.

- What did I do today that I could have done differently?
- What did I do that I could have done better?
- What did I not do that I could have done?

The process of qualification

There are three stages.

1   *Registration*

The NVQ/SVQ worker will be registered with an awarding body and will normally relate to a mentor or supervisor and be issued with a workbook. The assessor and an internal verifier will need to validate entries made in the workbook. There will also be an external verifier, whose task is to sample the work and advise on the work of assessment. In some cases they will get involved in the process of registering or deregistering a centre.

The assessment centre will produce two kinds of document, *formative logs* and *summative sheets*. The candidates normally use these to record evidence of their competence, unless they have had alternative documents approved by the centre, for their use.

2   *Collecting evidence for assessment*

Evidence is collected by four main means:

(a) observation of performance on the job;
(b) performance in a simulated job situation;
(c) oral questioning;
(d) written assignments on a topic.

3   *Being assessed as competent*

This requires a judgement of the evidence collected. Criteria need to ensure that the evidence is relevant, sufficient and valid. Here are some key criteria, expressed in the form of a checklist of questions.

- Does the worker demonstrate an acceptable standard of competence in the work done and how it is done?
- Can the worker describe and explain how the work was done?
- Can the worker produce appropriate written evidence, documenting the work done?

Assessment of competence is carried out by an assessment centre. This is a workplace that has been approved for this purpose. An NVQ/SVQ assessment centre may be all or part of a social services department in a local authority, a district health service, or one or more educational institutions in a partnership or a consortium with one or more of these. An assessment centre may also be a hospital or a trust in the health field. In the field of social care, the small size of many of the establishments in the voluntary or private sectors, in particular, makes it unlikely that units such as these would be assessment centres in their own right.

For General Level 3 in SVQs, direct work experience is not necessary, as it is largely classroom-based.

Assessment takes place through assessment centres. An assessment centre consists of the Joint Awarding Body. Staff include an external verifier, internal verifier and work-based assessor. Assessors are appointed by approved assessment centres. An assessor may be a co-worker, a line manager acting as supervisor, or a supervisor who is not the line manager. The job of the assessor is to collect evidence of competence in a variety of ways, based on how the candidate works.

Key questions

Use these questions to check back over the material covered in the chapter and assess your grasp of it, before moving on. Discuss the questions, and responses to them, with colleagues and tutors.

- ○ What are the main components of competent work with people?
- ○ What are the main strengths and weaknesses of the NVQ/SVQ approach?
- ○ What are the main differences between NVQ/SVQ Levels 2 and 4?
- ○ What items would you include in your CV?
- ○ What are the main barriers to unqualified workers gaining a qualification in work with people?
- ○ What are the main stages in the process of qualification, using NVQs/SVQs?

Further reading

On learning and study skills
Freeman, R. and Meed, J. (1993) *How to Study Effectively* (1993) National Extension College / Collins Educational.

Lewis, R. (forthcoming) *How to Manage Your Study Time*, National Extension College / Collins Educational.

Lewis, R. and Inglis, J. (forthcoming) *How to Manage Your Study Time*, National Extension College / Collins Educational.

Rowntree, D. (1990) *Learn How to Study: A Guide for Students of All Ages*, London: MacDonald.

For help with demonstrating competence in an NVQ
Meteyard, B. (1992) *Getting Started with NVQ: Tackling the Integrated Care Awards*, Harlow: Longman.

For an example of the competence-based approach
Sargeant, T., *et al.* (1992) *Field Support Workers: Feasibility Study for the Care Sector Consortium*, Manchester: Manchester Polytechnic.

For critical discussion of the NVQ approach
Kelly, D., Payne, C. and Warwick, J. (1990) *Making National Vocational Qualifications Work for Social Care*, London: National Institute for Social Work / Social Care Association.

References

Audit Commission (1989) The Probation Service: Promoting Value for Money, London: HMSO.

Beresford, P. and Croft, S. (1993) Citizen Involvement: A Practical Guide for Change, London: Macmillan.

Campbell, B. (1984) Wigan Pier Revisited: Poverty and Politics in the 80s, London: Virago.

Care Sector Consortium (1991) National Occupational Standards for Working with Young Children and Their Families, London: HMSO.

Care Sector Consortium (1992) National Occupational Standards for Care, London: HMSO.

CCETSW (1993) Assessment Documentation for Awards in Criminal Justice Services at Level III (CCETSW 29.3c) and Level IV (CCETSW 29.4e), London: Central Council for Education and Training in Social Work.

Clough, R. (1981) Old Age Homes, NISW Social Services Library No. 42, London: Allen & Unwin.

Darvill, G. and Smale, G. (eds) (1990) Partners in Empowerment: Networks of Innovation in Social Work, London: National Institute for Social Work.

DHSS (1980) Report of the Review of Rampton Hospital (Boynton Report), Cmnd 8073, London: HMSO.

Douglas, R. and Payne, C. (1991) Learning About Caring: An Introductory Package for Staff Development in Residential and Day Care Work, Section B, Practice Guides 1–4, London: National Institute for Social Work.

Grimwood, C. and Popplestone, R. (1993) Women, Management and Care, London: Macmillan.

Health and Safety Commission (1992) Management of Health and Safety at Work, SI 1992, no. 2051, London: HMSO.

Health and Safety Executive (1992) Manual Handling Operations Regulations, London: HMSO.

Home Office (1988) Punishment, Custody and the Community, Cmnd 424, London: HMSO.

King, R.D. and Morgan, R. (1976) A Taste of Prison: Custodial Conditions for Trial and Remand Prisoners, London: Routledge.

Kubler-Ross, E. (1981) Living with Death and Dying, London: Souvenir Press.

Levy, A. and Kahan, B. (1991) The Pindown Experience and the Protection of Children: The Report of the Staffordshire Child Care Inquiry 1990, Staffordshire: Staffs County Council.

Littlewood, J. (1992) Aspects of Grief: Bereavement in Adult Life, London: Routledge.

London Borough of Lambeth(1987) Whose Child? The Report of the Public Inquiry into the Death of Tyra Henry, London: London Borough of Lambeth.

Marris, P. (1992) Loss and Change, London: Routledge.

Morris, J. (1993) Pride Against Prejudice: Transforming Attitudes to Disability, London: Women's Press.

Payne, C. and Scott, T. (1985) Developing Supervision of Teams in Field and Residential Social Work, NISW Papers No. 17, London: National Institute for Social Work.

Rosenbaum, M. and Newell, P. (1991) Taking Children Seriously: A Proposal for a Children's Rights Commissioner, London: Calouste Gulbenkian Foundation.

Schon, D.A. (1991) The Reflective Practitioner: How Professionals Think in Action, Aldershot: Avebury.

Scottish Home and Health Department (1985) Report of the Review of Suicide Precautions at HM Detention Centre and HM Young Offenders Institution, Glenochil, London: HMSO.

Smale, G. and Ivson, G. with Biehal, N. and Marsh, P. (1993) Empowerment, Assessment, Care Management and the Skilled Worker, London: HMSO.

SSI (Social Services Inspectorate) (1987) From Home Help to Home Care: An Analysis of Policy, Resourcing and Service Management, London: HMSO.

SSI (1988) Managing Policy Change in Home Help Services, London: HMSO.

SSI (1989) Managing Home Care in Metropolitan Districts, London: HMSO.

SSI (1990) Inspecting Home Care Services: A Guide to the SSI Method, London: HMSO.

SSI (1991) Women in Social Services: A Neglected Resource, London: HMSO.

Street, D., Vinter, R.D. and Perrow, R.C. (1966) Organization for Treatment: A Comparative Study of Institutions for Delinquents, New York: Free Press.

Tomlinson, D.F. (1993) No Longer Afraid: The Safeguard of Older People in Domestic Settings, London: HMSO.

UNICEF (undated) New Dimensions, Fair Conditions, London: United Nations Children's Fund.

Utting, W. (1991) Children in the Public Care: A Review of Residential Child Care, London: HMSO.

Wertheimer, A. (ed.) (1991) A Chance to Speak Out: Consulting Service Users and Carers about Community Care, London: King's Fund Centre.

Winn, L. (ed.) (1992) Power to the People: The Key to Responsive Services in Health and Social Care, London: King's Fund.

Useful addresses

On NVQs

The Joint Awarding Bodies
Division 22
City and Guilds
46 Britannia Street
London
WC1X 9RG

On SVQs

SCOTVEC
Hanover House
124 Douglas Street
Glasgow
G2 7NQ

On healthy and hygienic environments

Health Education Authority
Hamilton House
Mabledon Place
London
WC1H 9TX

Health Research Board
73 Lower Baggot Street
Dublin 2

Health Education Board for Scotland
Woodburn House
Canaan Lane
Edinburgh
EG10 4SG

Health Promotion Authority for Wales
Brunel House
2 Fitzalan Road
Cardiff
CF2 1EB

Library of Health and Safety Executive
Broad Lane
Sheffield
S3 7HQ
Tel. 0742 768141

On managing diversity and other materials on management

Domino Consultancy Ltd
139 Ashby Road
Loughborough
Leics
LE11 OBR

On work with children under five

Pre-school Playgroups Association
61–62 Kings Cross Road
London
WC1X 9LL

National Children's Bureau
8 Wakley Street
London
EC1V 7QE

For complaints about services, not satisfied by service providers

Local Ombudsman
21 Queen Anne's Gate
London
SW1H 9BU

Index